STATE SCHOOLS

Woburn Education Series

General Series Editor: Professor Peter Gordon

For over 20 years this series on the history, development and policy of education, under the distinguished editorship of Peter Gordon, has been evolving into a comprehensive and balanced survey of important trends in teaching and educational policy. The series is intended to reflect the changing nature of education in present-day society. The books are divided into four sections – educational policy studies, educational practice, the history of education and social history – and reflect the continuing interest in this area.

For a full series listing, please visit our website: www.woburnpress.com

HISTORY OF EDUCATION

The Victorian School Manager: A Study in the Management of Education 1800–1902
Peter Gordon

Selection for Secondary Education
Peter Gordon

The Study of Education: Inaugural Lectures
Volume I: Early and Modern
Volume II: The Last Decade
Volume III: The Changing Scene
Volume IV: End of an Era?
edited by Peter Gordon

History of Education: the Making of a Discipline
edited by Peter Gordon and Richard Szreter

Educating the Respectable: A Study of Fleet Road Board School, Hampstead, 1879–1903
W.E. Marsden

In History and in Education: Essays Presented to Peter Gordon
edited by Richard Aldrich

An Anglo-Welsh Teaching Dynasty: the Adams Family from the 1840s to the 1930s
W.E. Marsden

Dictionary of British Educationists
Richard Aldrich and Peter Gordon

Biographical Dictionary of North American and European Educationists
Peter Gordon and Richard Aldrich

Her Majesty's Inspectorate of Schools since 1944: Standard Bearers or Turbulent Priests?
John Dunford

STATE SCHOOLS

New Labour and the Conservative Legacy

Edited by

CLYDE CHITTY

and

JOHN DUNFORD

WOBURN PRESS

LONDON • PORTLAND, OR

First published in 1999 in Great Britain by
WOBURN PRESS
Newbury House
900 Eastern Avenue
London IG2 7HH

and in the United States of America by
WOBURN PRESS
c/o ISBS
5804 N.E. Hassalo Street
Portland, Oregon 97213-3644

Website: www.woburnpress.com

British Library Cataloguing in Publication Data:
State Schools: New Labour and Conservative legacy. –
(The Woburn education series)
1. Education and state – England 2. Education and state
– Wales
I. Chitty, Clyde II. Dunford, John
379'.0942

ISBN: 978-0-7130-4034-0

Library of Congress Cataloging-in-Publication Data:
State schools: new Labour and Conservative legacy / edited by
Clyde Chitty and John Dunford.
p. cm. – (Woburn education series)
Includes bibliographical references (p.) and index.
ISBN 0-7130-0214-X (cloth). – ISBN 0-7130-4034-3 (paper)
Public schools – Political aspects – Great Britain. 2. Education
and state – Great Britain. I. Chitty, Clyde. II. Dunford, J. E.
III. Series.
LC93.G7S73 1999
371.01'0941–DC21 99–28050
CIP

CONTENTS

ABBREVIATIONS

BTEC	Business and Technician (later, Technology) Education Council
CPD	Continuing Professional Development
CPVE	Certificate of Pre-Vocational Education
CSE	Certificate of Secondary Education
DES	Department of Education and Science
DF	Devolved Funding
DFE	Department for Education
DfEE	Department for Education and Employment
DoVE	Diploma of Vocational Education
GCE	General Certificate of Education
GCSE	General Certificate of Secondary Education
GM	Grant-Maintained [School]
GNVQ	General National Vocational Qualification
GTC	General Teaching Council
HMI	Her or His Majesty's Inspectorate
HOD	Head of Department
HOF	Head of Faculty
ICT	Information and Communications Technology
ILEA	Inner London Education Authority
ILTA	Inner London Teachers' Association
LEA	Local Education Authority
LSI	Local Schools Information
NASUWT	National Association of Schoolmasters/Union of Women Teachers
NCC	National Curriculum Council

NCVQ	National Council for Vocational Qualifications
NVQ	National Vocational Qualification
NUT	National Union of Teachers
Ofsted	Office for Standards in Education
PTA	Parent–Teacher Association
SAT	Standard Assessment Test
SCAA	School Curriculum and Assessment Authority
SCDC	Schools Curriculum Development Council
SEAC	School Examination and Assessment Council
SEC	Schools Examination Council
SHA	Secondary Heads Association
TTA	Teacher Training Agency
TVEI	Technical and Vocational Education Initiative

1

INTRODUCTION

JOHN DUNFORD AND CLYDE CHITTY

It has not been easy working in state schools since 1979. Throughout a period of nearly 20 years, the failings of state schools have been widely publicised while their successes have largely been belittled. The Conservative Government displayed remarkably little confidence in the state system that it was statutorily obliged to administer. One of the aims of this book is to trace the development of this phenomenon and to show, mainly from the perspective of the headteachers, what it has been like to work in and lead state schools during this period. But headteachers are largely optimistic people – they need to be – and so this book looks forward as well as back, analysing the agenda for the Labour Government in the light of the legacy left by its predecessor.

A LACK OF COMMITMENT

Conservative Education Ministers have consistently shown a lack of commitment towards the state system. This is hardly surprising when, for example, Mark Carlisle (Secretary of State, 1979–81) has said: 'I had no direct knowledge of the state sector either as a pupil or as a parent' (Ribbins and Sherratt, 1997, p. 55). His successor, Sir Keith Joseph, (Secretary of State, 1981–86) was even more dismissive:

> When I started the job in September 1981, I was anxious to free up the system, to free it from unnecessary bureaucratic controls ... I've always been attracted to the idea of the education voucher and I've always

> worried about the state's involvement in education. That had also been one of my chief concerns as Secretary of State for Industry. I thought there was a strong ideological case for abolishing the Department of Industry altogether, since really the state has no business getting involved in industry. We do not know how to go about it. And it's the same with education. We have a bloody state system; I wish we hadn't got one. I wish we'd taken a different route in 1870. We got the ruddy state involved. I don't want it. I don't think we know how to do it. I certainly don't think Secretaries of State know anything about it. But we are landed with it. (Chitty in Ribbins and Sherratt, 1997, p. 80)

One of the first acts of the new Thatcher administration in 1979 was to introduce the assisted places scheme, with the implication that 'bright' children had to be taken out of the state system and educated privately, and expensively, with the taxpayers paying the bill, in order to fulfil their educational potential. Gradually, over the following 18 years, the Conservatives' lack of commitment to comprehensive secondary schools became clearer, as ministers continually criticised these schools and created alternative forms of secondary school to undermine the integrity of the state system. Thus grant-maintained schools, city technology colleges and, eventually, attempts to increase the number of selective and specialist schools were introduced. Primary schools were not immune from this criticism, as sections of the media followed the lead of government ministers in attacking the system. Driving an even harder line than the ministers was a group of Conservative backbench Members of Parliament. They were closely connected with a number of right-wing pressure groups, such as the Centre for Policy Studies and the Institute of Economic Affairs, which played a crucial role in moving the political agenda further to the Right (Chitty, 1989; Knight, 1990). These groups also had an influential role in 10 Downing Street, being close to Prime Ministers Thatcher and Major as well as to their immediate advisers on education policy. The relationship between Downing Street and the Education Department during this period will make interesting reading when the private papers are published in 30 years' time.

A LACK OF TRUST

From the schools' perspective, it seemed that the Conservative Government did not trust teachers. Their attitude towards doctors during Kenneth Clarke's period as Health Minister suggested that this may have been part of a wider distrust of the professions, but the consequences for headteachers were severe, as they found themselves leading staffrooms with low morale and falling self-esteem. The teachers' action in the mid-1980s, although falling short of all-out strike, had a profound effect, lasting well beyond the action itself, both within schools and on the public perception of the teaching profession. Emily Blatch, later, as Baroness Blatch, to be Minister of State in the Department for Education, often recalled the effect of the teachers' action at Hinchingbrooke School, Huntingdon, on the education of her children.

It was in this atmosphere that Joseph wanted to introduce a punitive model of teacher appraisal and it proved impossible for those who wanted to create a General Teaching Council, similar to that in Scotland, to persuade the Government that the profession should have this degree of self-control. Consultation on all new education legislation was perfunctory, often taking place during the summer months when most teachers were away on holiday. This was particularly so during the preparations for the introduction of the National Curriculum in 1987; it was only when Sir Ron Dearing was asked in 1993 to put right the disastrous consequences of this failure to involve the profession that genuine consultation took place.

Her Majesty's Inspectorate (HMI) was not seen by the teachers as being especially friendly towards them, but rather as a body which was even-handed in its criticism, reporting as it found and criticising schools and the Government in equal measure. Kenneth Clarke (Secretary of State, 1990–92) saw HMI as being too close to the teachers and delivering too many messages uncomfortable to the Government. His reform of HMI and the creation of Ofsted effectively turned the inspectors' fire almost entirely on to the teachers and away from the Government.

THE DECLINING ROLE OF LOCAL EDUCATION AUTHORITIES (LEAs)

The abolition of the Inner London Education Authority (ILEA) appeared to be part of a wider programme of reform designed to reduce the powers of local education authorities. This movement was fuelled by a highly political campaign, centred on a number of London boroughs, attempting to discredit Labour local authorities and to imply that they were controlled by the so-called 'loony left'. No longer could state education be described, as it had been for 60 years, as a three-way partnership between central government, local government and the schools themselves. The powers of the LEAs were reduced and, from the schools' viewpoint, the service which they provided was changed beyond recognition. If the 1980s was a bad time to be working in state schools, it was even worse for those working in local authorities.

CENTRALISATION AND DECENTRALISATION

The great paradox of the Conservative Government's period of office was the simultaneous introduction of both greater centralisation and greater decentralisation. It was as if the lack of trust in teachers led the Government to measures of centralisation such as the National Curriculum and Ofsted (Office for Standards in Education), while their lack of trust in local authorities led to decentralisation measures such as local management of schools and grant-maintained status. Kenneth Clarke explained the paradox on the grounds that the Government needed to describe the framework for state education, but that it wished the people on the ground to deliver it and be accountable for their success in doing so (Ribbins and Sherratt, 1997, p. 151).

The period from 1979 until 1986 had seen an increase in activity on the part of the Department of Education and Science (DES) and headteachers were already beginning to complain that they did not have enough time to read all that was being published by the Department and HMI. However, this was a mere trickle in comparison with the torrent of legislation and circulars which emanated from the Department after 1986. The extent of change in the education service was without precedent and headteachers had to act as 'sieves' in order to protect their staff from professional suffocation by innovation. Only in this way could schools continue to concentrate on the centrally important tasks of teaching and learning. Not all headteachers managed this successfully and the number of breakdowns and premature retirements among heads and teachers increased dramatically.

After 1986 much of this legislative hyperactivity transferred power from the DES to non-governmental bodies (quangos) such as the National Curriculum Council (NCC) and the School Examinations and Assessment Council (SEAC). For a Government which had taken office with the intention of reducing the number of quangos, this represented a major change of policy, but it enabled Ministers to exercise control over a much wider range of activity as the bodies were largely advisory and dependent on ministerial approval for the measures which they recommended. As Duncan Graham, the first chair and chief executive of the NCC has written, the civil servants who were responsible for the liaison between the Department and the quangos offered a further tier of control (Graham and Tytler, 1993, pp. 12ff.). Ministers also had the power of nomination of the members of the councils of the quangos and they frequently nominated individuals from the right-wing pressure groups mentioned above. With their close connections to ministers, and even to the Prime Minister, these people were extremely influential on the quangos which increasingly ruled over the educational landscape. It seemed that the 'loony left' local education authorities had been marginalised in order that the 'loony right' could, through their membership of quangos, dictate what state schools had to do.

THE MARKET

Sir Keith Joseph's views on the inappropriateness of the state's role in education stemmed from his market-oriented philosophy, which was so influential on Margaret Thatcher's premiership. Standards were to be driven up by market forces, of which the most significant measures were parental choice (more correctly, parental preference) of school, together with open enrolment and intake numbers for each school statutorily increased to their peak 1979 level. The publication of HMI reports on individual schools from 1983 and, later, the more frequent Ofsted reports were to give parents the information on which to base their choices. Headteachers had little alternative but to 'market' their schools and to compete with neighbouring schools for the attention of potential pupils and their parents. Some heads were good at it, some complained that this was not what they had come into teaching for, but all had to learn fast, especially when local management of schools was introduced and the financial viability of the school came to depend almost entirely on the number of pupils recruited.

The publication of examination performance tables made the situation more acute and was especially difficult for schools in areas of social deprivation, on which the pressure became intense. The cycle of poor examination results, smaller intake numbers, less finance and fewer teachers created enormous pressure on the teaching staff and particularly on the head and senior staff, many of whom chose to end their careers prematurely.

SUCCESSFUL SCHOOLS

In spite of this recurring problem, state schools were extremely successful between 1979 and 1997. In 1979, 25 per cent of 16 year olds passed at least five GCE Ordinary levels ('O' levels); in 1997 the equivalent figure for GCSE examination grades A* (i.e. above A grade) to C was 45 per cent. At GCE Advanced level ('A' level), the percentage of 18 year olds passing in at least two subjects rose from 14 to 28 per cent. In 1979, 12 per cent of the 18-year-old age cohort entered higher education; by 1997 this figure had risen to over 30 per cent. Right-wing critics of state education complained that these increases were caused by falling standards in public examinations, but they never managed to prove this and independent studies failed to support the case for falling standards.

During this period there was only a small growth in the percentage of school-age children at independent schools and the proportion at boarding schools decreased. Thus state schools held their place against the challenge of independent schools during a period when the relative expenditure per pupil, and hence the class size, increasingly favoured independent schools.

The success of Scottish state schools continued during the 1980s and 1990s. The proportion of children at Scottish independent schools was only 3 per cent and the remaining 97 per cent were all educated at comprehensive primary and secondary schools. The post-16 participation rate, the proportion of the cohort entering higher education and other performance indicators remained, throughout the period, higher in Scotland than in England and Wales. There has never been any doubt of the fervent support of Scottish people for their education system and this commitment extended right up to the Scottish Office and the Scottish HMI, who continue to play an important role in all the developments in Scottish education.

FROM OPPOSITION TO GOVERNMENT

One of the frustrations for school leaders was the ineffectiveness of the Opposition to the Conservative policies. The Government, for most of the period, had a clear, radical vision and introduced policies which were consistent with this philosophy. It was the Government which was setting the pace and the Opposition seemed to be able to do little other than oppose. The Labour Party, and to a lesser extent the Liberal Democrats, were constantly in reactive mode, appearing to defend the status quo and generally failing to put forward clear alternative policies. Towards the end of the period, the opposition parties began to develop a more coherent set of policies, but they failed to transmit them effectively to the electorate before the 1997 general election campaign.

When Gillian Shephard was Secretary of State and David Blunkett was

Labour spokesperson, the policies of the two main parties became indistinguishable in many areas, as the general election neared and the parties sought to occupy the centre ground. However, the right-wing pressure on Mrs Shephard to introduce nursery vouchers and more selective schooling identified the topics on which the election was fought. On the central issue of school standards, there was little difference between the parties.

On taking office, the Labour Government had a huge agenda. This had been itemised in its manifesto during an election campaign in which Labour leader Tony Blair declared that 'education, education and education' were to be the top three priorities of his Government. This created enormous pressure on David Blunkett and his ministerial team to produce policies on a wide range of issues, including standards of achievement, class size, the structure of schools, pre-school provision, children with special educational needs and the role of local education authorities. Outside the school sector, they also had to face the thorny issues, avoided by the previous Government, arising from the grave financial difficulties into which both universities and further education colleges had fallen.

The Education Ministers were also charged by the Prime Minister with the more sensitive and difficult task of altering the balance between pressure and support on schools, aiming to provide a more supportive atmosphere while continuing the previous Government's drive to raise standards of achievement in schools. This was to provide the first major difficulty for the new Government when, after immediate and widely welcomed policy declarations on the abolition of nursery vouchers and the assisted places scheme, the Minister of State, Stephen Byers, named the 18 'worst performing schools'. This represented a clear sign that, whatever measures were to be put in place to support schools in difficulties, pressure would continue to be applied. Most of the schools were, not surprisingly, serving socially deprived communities where the problems are much wider than education alone.

Sir Keith Joseph often spoke about the 'bottom 40 per cent', correctly identifying one of the major problem areas for state schools, but not knowing what measures to introduce in order to solve the problem. Over a decade later, this remains one of the major challenges for the Labour Government and, without a solution to this problem, national achievement targets will not be met.

As the external pressures on schools have grown in the early 1990s, the number of pupils excluded from schools, especially secondary schools, has grown by several hundred per cent. Parental rights have grown, without a concomitant rise in their responsibilities for the education of the child. Consequently, the range of sanctions available to schools has decreased and the ultimate sanction of exclusion has been reached much earlier in the disciplinary process. This has created an underclass of excluded teenagers, who are at the most problematic end of Joseph's '40 per cent'.

Low morale in the teaching force and, closely related to this, the crisis in teacher supply, which strikes first in the very areas where social conditions are most difficult, are perhaps the thorniest problems which the Government has to face. Legislation can be introduced on many issues, but problems of teacher morale and supply cannot be solved by statute.

One of the most worrying features of the Labour Government's education policy is the underlying assumption that all problems can be solved at the centre. The Labour Party, which criticised the Conservatives for being so centralist, has produced legislation which extends the power of the state – and particularly of the Secretary of State for Education and Employment – still further. Lord Pilkington, speaking in the House of Lords during the second reading of the Teaching and Higher Education Bill, commented: 'So many powers are reserved in the Bill to the Secretary of State that, in contrast, the dictatorial Statute of Proclamations of Henry VIII looks like an almost amateur effort in control' (*Times Educational Supplement*, 19 December 1997). If teacher morale is to be improved and teacher supply is to increase with a stream of high quality graduate trainees, teachers must be empowered, not controlled from the centre. A stronger General Teaching Council – instead of the weak GTC which has been proposed – and a greater emphasis on quality assurance through school self-evaluation, rather than quality control through Ofsted, would provide two important signs of the change in direction which is required.

School leaders want the Government to succeed in creating a state education system of which the whole country is proud. We want ministers to work with us, and not against us, in this crusade. If this happens, then we shall see the improvement in teacher morale on which the educational edifice can be strongly built. Parts of the Conservative legacy have provided the Government with the foundations on which to base some of its policies, but part of the legacy undermines state schools and their teachers. The following chapters contain many proposals on how the process of reform and reconstruction can be accomplished.

2

THE CHANGING PRESSURES ON PRIMARY SCHOOLS

C. ERIC SPEAR

In the late 1990s it is a commonplace to suppose that standards of education have fallen and that schools are to blame for a lack of rigour and plain common sense. In particular, primary schools have come in for criticism, even sometimes from their secondary school colleagues, for failing to teach the basics of numeracy and literacy adequately. Politicians affect to fear that there lurks in every school a core of trendy, woolly minded liberals, determined to undermine the values and standards of traditional society.

Sir David Eccles, Conservative Minister of Education from 1959 to 1962, referred to 'the secret garden of the curriculum', during a 1960 House of Commons debate on the Crowther Report, and this was the first straw in the wind that politicians were becoming uneasy about the autonomy which schools enjoyed over the school curriculum. As late as 1970, however, it was still true to affirm 'that nowhere else in the world does a teacher have so much freedom in the choice of what to teach as he [*sic*] does in Britain' (Wiseman and Pidgeon, 1970, p. 9).

The subsequent, increasing focus on the end-products of secondary education, raising the school-leaving age and unifying the national examination at 16, increasing the staying-on rate post-16 and the expansion plans for higher education, left primary schools largely free from direct political interference for a while. In the late 1950s and early 1960s, there was a great upsurge of new ideas and experimentation in teaching methodology, designed to make learning more responsive to pupils' needs and to make it more attractive to learn. This movement predated by a decade the Plowden Report (DES, 1967), which gave it the seal of approval. However, the issue was still one of methodology, not content. There was little debate about what should be taught.

But even as the Plowden Report was published, voices were raised questioning the new orthodoxy. The Black Papers of the late 1960s and 1970s, produced by a number of right-wing educationists and commentators, polarised the debate in terms of 'traditional' versus 'progressive' teaching methods and advocated a return to the methods and disciplines of traditional teaching. But other aspects of schooling were becoming the subject of debate. Early in the curriculum debate, John White was one of the few educational philosophers to examine the notion of a minimum core curriculum for all: 'In any rational education system . . . it is of paramount importance to determine this basic minimum. It is a reflection on the British educational system that it does not attempt to do this' (White, 1973, p. 1).

While many voices were raised in defence of liberty and choice and warnings were issued on the dangers of a centrally prescribed curriculum becoming the tool of a totalitarian regime, elsewhere some schools were offering ammunition to the proponents of a centralised curriculum.

In 1975 the educational world was rocked by the William Tyndale Schools affair – where it was claimed that a number of so-called 'progressive' primary school teachers had been allowed to operate an extreme version of child-centred education – and the subsequent Auld Inquiry Report (1976) helped to spark the Great Education Debate, launched by Prime Minister James Callaghan in his 1976 Ruskin College speech. Suddenly the gloves were off. Every aspect of education was now under scrutiny, and government intervention seemed necessary to tackle a national system, locally administered, which was universally suspected of having failed at a variety of levels.

At the end of 1978, the DES published the first of a series of reports on the state of education. *Primary Education in England* focused mainly on the junior, 7–11, range, now known as key stage 2.[1] Its Foreword contained the beginnings of an agenda for primary education which has not yet been fully worked through: 'teachers in primary schools work hard to make pupils well-behaved, literate and numerate. They are concerned for individual children, especially for those who find it difficult to learn' (DES, 1978). While finding that reading test results for 11 year olds were 'encouraging', it noted the absence of 'objective evidence of past standards in other parts of the curriculum', and observed that 'in some aspects of the work, the results overall are sometimes disappointing . . . the evidence clearly suggests that difficulties arise because individual teachers are trying to cover too much unaided'. It went on to hint at the need for specialisation. Ironically, even after a major Education Act and numerous smaller ones, that observation remains valid. Indeed, a rereading of the report 20 years later highlights all the major issues affecting primary education with which we have subsequently become familiar. They include the identification of curriculum coordinators and specialists in primary schools, better planning of the content and range of the curriculum, the extension of the more able child and, prophetically, the suggestion that whole-class teaching was sometimes a more efficient use of teacher time.

PRIMARY SCHOOLS IN THE LATE 1970s

It is difficult for the present generation of new teachers to imagine what it was like to teach in primary schools 20 years ago, so it is worth recalling some of the major features.

There was no requirement to teach any subject except religious education. Schools determined their own curriculum and HMI would later claim that this led to idiosyncratic curricular decisions, although perhaps we have since learned to call that 'choice and diversity' and have seen it as an advantage. The abolition in most parts of the country of the 11-plus selection examination determining entry to grammar or secondary modern schools, together with the publication of the Plowden Report had given primary schools the freedom to throw off the remaining shackles of the Victorian elementary tradition, with its narrow, uninspiring focus on the 'three Rs'. The Wilson Government's pledge to engage in the 'white heat of technology', the increasingly rapid changes in the demands from industry and the patterns of future employment, signalled the need for a style of education which went far beyond the basics. Indeed, it was becoming clear that the principal job of schools was to equip pupils with the ability and the desire to continue their learning for life. The future needs of society were no longer predictable, as they had seemed only a generation ago.

In-service teacher education was much more ad hoc than it is today, and its provision relied more on individual initiative than upon any structure for identifying individual and institutional needs. The concept of school development planning was little understood or practised, and there were few of the demands and initiatives to which we have since become accustomed.

The powers of governors were greater than most supposed, but were rarely exercised and governors played little part in the day-to-day life of most schools.

Finance was controlled almost entirely by the LEA, which was responsible for the employment and dismissal of staff, although, until the 1980s, there was very little of the latter. Schools had little control over their own destinies and had little opportunity to use their own resources creatively.

A UNIFIED AND CENTRALISED SYSTEM

The 1988 Education Reform Act laid down in considerable detail how education should be managed and conducted. It allowed the Secretary of State to introduce a compulsory National Curriculum and ushered in local management of schools. A system of pupil testing and public accountability ensured that schools were not able to ignore the implications of the Act. The subsequent setting up of the Office for Standards in Education (Ofsted), with published inspection reports on each school every four years, handed the Government a powerful influence over the work of schools. Indeed it has been said that the powers granted by legislation in 1988, and subsequently, made the Secretary of State for Education the envy of totalitarian regimes throughout the world.

The 1988 Act imposed upon primary schools an unmanageable, subject-based curriculum; a cumbersome and unworkable assessment system which eventually led to the publication of key stage 2 assessment results; and the public 'naming and shaming' of schools which came bottom of the 'league tables' of results. A pupil-number-driven budget encouraged schools to compete for pupils and undermined the spirit of cooperation which had previously been regarded as a major strength of the system.

Subsequent tinkering with the system has somewhat ameliorated the worst effects of this legislation but has left teachers feeling that the ground is forever moving beneath their feet. The effect on morale has been so severe that the last Government had to change the rules for premature retirement because so many teachers were using it to escape the unacceptable stress of the job they had once enjoyed.

A change of government has not improved matters. In fact it has given renewed impetus for change during a period when the last government had promised a five-year moratorium on new initiatives. The documentation overload stacks up unabated and there is a growing crisis in teacher supply. The pressures of managing an under-resourced system and the increasing conflicts with governing bodies, which have begun to exercise their power, have led to a significant shortage of candidates for headship and deputy headship.

There has long been a funding crisis in education and it has always been felt worst at primary level. None of the initiatives of the last ten years has been adequately funded and schools have had to reduce staffing to a minimum, and thus increase class sizes, in order to balance budgets.

Now primary schools are facing a very public challenge, offered by the new Secretary of State, David Blunkett. By 2002, 80 per cent of children should achieve a standard of literacy considered average by today's standards and 75 per cent should achieve a similar standard in numeracy.

The new Labour Government has promised that its priorities will be 'education, education and education', as the Prime Minister, Tony Blair, announced. So what should schools be hoping for in the new millennium?

BEYOND 2000 – THE FUTURE OF PRIMARY EDUCATION

In Africa, as the saying goes, all you need to start a school is a blackboard, a shady tree and a teacher. If we interpret the shady tree to mean a suitable environment and the blackboard to be basic equipment, then the same holds true anywhere in the world. The essential requirement in all cases is a good teacher. A supply of well-educated, well-motivated and professionally well-prepared teachers is crucial to the success of any educational reform and for the achievement of improved standards of pupil attainment.

Such improvements cannot be achieved merely by tinkering with structures and legislating for curriculum content and method. Teacher-proofing the school system has been tried in the past and has been abandoned because it minimises the use of the most expensive, adaptable and creative resource of the school.

The present picture of teacher recruitment is not encouraging and the number of men training for the primary phase is tiny. The current under-achievement of boys in primary schools is beginning to be blamed on the shortage of male role models, leading to the impression among boys that activities such as reading are exclusively female occupations. The image of a beleaguered profession, the victim of both government denigration and a concerted press campaign alleging falling standards, does nothing to raise the image of teaching at any level.

A sustained campaign to raise teachers' morale and their professional image is needed. The Government has already recognised this in its cinema and TV advertising campaign, but has failed to realise that it is how teachers are treated which forms the most potent image in the mind of the public. The more credible, current image of teachers is of a stressed, harassed and harried workforce losing control of its professional destiny.

SPECIALIST TEACHERS

There is a particular need to recruit primary teachers with specialist subject knowledge to allow the 'more able' pupils at the top end of key stage 2 to be extended. This can be achieved, however, only if primary schools are staffed differently from the traditional one-teacher, one-class model which we inherited from the Victorian elementary school tradition. To a Victorian, transported into our time, one of the most striking aspects of modern primary school organisation would be its familiarity! If specialists are to be effective, they will need to be *additional* to the existing staff, so that they not only teach children but work alongside class teachers to enhance their skills as well. The Government's proposal for a grade of advanced skills teacher is merely a palliative, which is likely to do more harm than good in the short term. Few schools, for example, will want to lose their best teachers for a day or more each week to other schools, as is proposed, and few schools will be able to pay the sort of salaries being proposed for these teachers, unless extra resources are provided for the purpose.

Schools' own specialist teachers would need access to specialist facilities as well, with rooms equipped for science and technology, for example. Time is the scarcest commodity teachers have and yet much of it is used in transferring computers, televisions and video players from one room to another. The 'high-tech' classroom of the future will have all this equipment installed permanently in every classroom.

The Government's latest initiative to link every school to the Internet and, by the year 2000, to have 75 per cent of teachers and 50 per cent of pupils fully computer-literate, is an ambitious target which, if achieved, may well give us a world lead in this area. It will, however, require a major diversion of school resources to fund it and without major, additional investment from government or industry, this is bound to be at the expense of other, equally worthwhile activities.

TARGETS AND SMALL MEASUREMENTS

The current government obsession with target-setting for improved numeracy and literacy amongst primary pupils by the year 2002 derives from the untested assumption that this will improve the reservoir of national skills and talent and, inevitably, national prosperity. However, as Dr Peter Robinson, of the Institute for Public Policy Research, has asked:

> how is it that the United States remains the world's most successful

> industrial nation when their pupils are no better at maths than the English? (*Times Educational Supplement*, 20 March 1998)

The belief that concentrating on the basic skills will somehow make us a more successful nation is an untested assumption. Target-setting also makes assumptions about what the basics of a good education are and accepts that these are entirely related to our economic performance as a nation.

One of the major concerns expressed about the Secretary of State's announcement in early 1998, concerning the five new core subjects of the primary school curriculum – English, maths, science, information technology and religious education – is that schools will be tempted to concentrate on these to the virtual exclusion of everything else, because that is where their accountability will be most tested.

There is a growing awareness, however, of the importance of the contribution of the arts in education, because they help to develop understanding of, and sensitivity to, the human condition and therefore play a vital role in the curriculum.

Similarly, there is growing concern about the physical health of children, who are observed to be more sedentary than previous generations, even in the playground. Because they are taken everywhere by car, often for reasons of security, children have less exercise than their parents did and spend a great deal of time in front of television and computer screens, a situation that will worsen if the Government's world-wide learning web initiative proves to be successful. Primary school children need regular physical activity to release the pent-up energy which otherwise often reveals itself in classroom disruption and inattention to task. Thus, although regular periods of physical education and games perform several valuable educational and health functions, they are in danger of being squeezed to make room for the statutory timetabling of literacy, numeracy and anything else the Government might decide in the future should become a national priority.

One of the great burdens which primary schools will carry into the next century is a preoccupation with testing and assessment. Few other countries have attempted the English and Welsh type of national testing on such a comprehensive scale or have made schools so publicly accountable for their results, especially at primary school level. Of course teachers find carefully validated standardised tests a useful moderator of their own professional judgements. Experienced teachers, who have always practised the assessment of their pupils in a systematic way, can be not only very accurate in their assessments, but also more comprehensive in their judgement of a child's all-round abilities and in forecasting the child's future educational needs. If we are going to rely on the published test results of the easily measurable parts of only certain subjects in the curriculum to validate a school's success, then we are in danger of impoverishing teaching and learning by focusing on the testable. We will end up knowing 'the price of everything and the value of nothing', as Oscar Wilde once said in a different context. Teaching to the test is not a new concept; we have been there before. It is one of the tragedies afflicting education that we seem to have to repeat the same mistakes in order to learn the same lessons. Denis Lawton has proposed that,

> In the long run there would be advantages in separating the two functions of assessment by returning to APU (Assessment and Performance Unit) testing (on the basis of light sampling, not testing every child) to monitor standards, and use national curriculum assessment for formative and diagnostic purposes. (Lawton, 1993, p. 68)

Although teacher assessment is supposed to have equal status with standard assessment test (SAT) results, people tend to trust the test results more because they are regarded as 'objective' and therefore 'accurate'. The track record of SATs at key stages 2 and 3 in particular leaves this contention open to doubt.

Teachers are becoming better at making judgements about children as they are compelled to do so by legislation and by parental clamour for information on their children's progress and perhaps, in the next century, some kind of portfolio of achievement will become the norm for primary schools, as it has for secondary schools over the last decade.

SCHOOL MANAGEMENT AND MONEY

As primary schools are organised and funded there is little time for management built into their structures. Meetings of key staff, and meetings between the head and individual teachers, necessarily take place outside lesson time because few primary teachers have 'non-contact' time. The environment of a school often conspires against good management. There are few offices or rooms where small meetings can take place in uninterrupted privacy and, where they exist, they are often overcrowded and ill equipped for the purpose. Money spent on management is minimised because finance is so short. Expenditure on anything other than children is regarded as an expensive and dispensable luxury. Many of the bad judgements we make are the result of inadequate consultation and of having insufficient time to reflect on the possible options and their consequences. If time is needed to ensure good planning and decision-making, then governors and heads must not feel guilty about paying for it. Government, both national and local, should recognise this in the allocation of funding to primary schools.

If standards of education are to be raised, not only do we need to recruit good teachers; we need to motivate and retain them. Part of being motivated is being well managed, so that teachers obtain feedback on their performance and support for their professional development. Such management cannot be achieved without non-contact time for heads and senior staff in large primary schools. The ability to watch teachers teach might be central to the current appraisal regulations, but it is also a necessary function of routine personnel management in a school. If it is to be productive, such observation needs to be routine and regular with adequate time for follow-up discussion between observer and observed. While the latter may be done out of school hours, the former can be done only in lesson time and this has implications for staffing levels in all primary schools. The only way to increase non-contact time in primary schools is to make a significant increase in their funding. To achieve adequate non-contact time for the monitoring and development of both teachers and the curriculum would require additional funding in the order of at least 10 per cent in the average primary school budget. This would fund, on average, half a day per week of non-contact time for every teacher, which could be used for a variety of necessary managerial functions at the discretion of the headteacher.

Primary school budgets will need to be enhanced to cope with the additional teachers needed and for the major investment expected in the next four years if schools are to achieve the information and communications technology (ICT) targets set by the Government. Tens of thousands of pounds per school will be needed to replace all the outdated computers which teachers have lovingly tended over the years and to add sufficiently to their number to offer adequate access to all pupils and teachers. Annual running and maintenance costs will be several thousands of pounds per year. These will be large, additional financial burdens on schools which have not yet emerged from the effects of several years of harsh economic settlements.

Schools also need to be funded on a basis which will allow them to take a medium-term view of their needs. The present annual view, afforded to schools halfway through each school year, does little to promote rational planning. An indicative budget for three years ahead would be a helpful strategy, and some way of lining up the financial and academic years should be considered.

The Commons Select Committee on Education and Employment is, at the time of writing, considering the role of the headteacher in schools. It is asking some radical questions about the nature of, and even the need for, headteachers. It is asking whether heads need to be teachers and whether 'captains of industry' might not perform better. It is considering the merits of 'super heads' being in charge of a cluster of schools, as seems to be intended in some of the newly defined Education Action Zones (see 'Conclusion' in this volume).

If the notion of headship is to be challenged in this way, then the financial and physical realities of management will have to be confronted. Captains of industry will not expect to share their office with the school secretary in a redundant Victorian classroom piled high with boxes of exercise books and pencils. They will certainly expect a company car and expenses if they are going to manage clusters of schools which might involve round trips of several miles. Perhaps funding a little extra time for existing management functions begins to look like an attractive alternative.

THE CHALLENGE

The Labour Government will have to do more than issue challenges to primary schools if we are to make the required improvements in the next four years. In particular, we need to secure an adequate supply of good quality teachers and enhance the staffing of primary schools to allow for smaller classes and teacher non-contact time. We need to improve the level of primary school funding and the system by which it is distributed and, at the same time, upgrade the physical facilities of primary schools to allow the proper teaching of subjects like science, technology and ICT. Above all, we need to be free of government interference for short-term political gain.

NOTE

1. Key stage 1 refers to the schooling of 5 to 7 year olds; key stage 2 to 7 to 11; key stage 3 to 11 to 14; key stage 4 to 14 to 16.

3

THE COMPREHENSIVE IDEAL

CLYDE CHITTY

For most of the twentieth century, Britain has had a highly stratified system of education based on the twin concepts of higher-status schooling for a select minority of pupils and lower-status provision for the rest. The 1944 Education Act appeared to organise British education in a more 'progressive' form than anything operating before the Second World War in that it sought to extend educational opportunity by providing free secondary education for all. Yet it had a number of serious weaknesses and shortcomings, not always recognised at the time and not least with regard to its ambiguity in certain key areas of provision. One such area concerned the exact structure of the secondary school system which would now embrace all state pupils over the age of 11. This was to be a cause of much debate and controversy in the post-war years.

The initial assumptions favoured a bipartite or tripartite system of secondary schools, even though multilateral and comprehensive schools were not officially proscribed in the Act. One interpretation of Section 8, referring to the provision of opportunities for all pupils 'in view of their different ages, abilities and aptitudes, and of the different periods for which they may be expected to remain at school', ensured that secondary reform of a radical nature was deferred for many years. At the same time, it can be argued that the ambiguity in the wording of this section meant that when the pressure for reform became almost irresistible in the 1960s, it could be carried out by *reinterpreting* the formula without any need for further legislation. Indeed, attention was drawn to this possibility, even while the Bill was under discussion, by an experienced educational administrator, J. Chuter Ede, the Labour Parliamentary Secretary to the Board of Education:

> I do not know where people get the idea about three types of school, because I have gone through the Bill with a small toothcomb, and I can find only one school for senior pupils – and that is a secondary school. What you like to make of it will depend on the way you serve the precise needs of the individual area in the country. (speech reported in *The Times*, 14 April 1944, quoted in Rubinstein and Simon, 1973, p. 31)

The movement to establish comprehensive schools in the 1950s was very much a grass-roots affair, with no encouragement, and often fierce opposition, from the Conservative Government, in power from 1951 to 1964. The last-minute intervention of the Minister of Education, Florence Horsbrugh, to prevent the London County Council (LCC) from closing the Eltham Hill Girls' Grammar School in 1954 and transferring the pupils to the new Kidbrooke School meant that London's first purpose-built comprehensive school was not as 'comprehensive' as it might have been. By 1960, the number of pupils in comprehensive schools in England and Wales still amounted to less than 5 per cent of the secondary school population (Benn and Simon, 1972, p. 102).

Yet it was, in fact, the period of the late 1950s and early 1960s when what C. P. Snow described (in his famous 1959 lecture on *The Two Cultures*) as 'the rigid and crystallised pattern' of English education was beginning to break up under the weight of its own contradictions. It was becoming obvious to large numbers of parents and politicians that far too many children were being written off as 'failures' at the age of 11 at a time when new demands were being made on the educational system as a result of technological change and economic advance. What was remarkable about the comprehensive ideal was its ability to secure converts from right across the political spectrum – a fact conveniently ignored by Conservative leaders in subsequent decades.

In an extraordinarily frank letter to Fred Jarvis, former General Secretary of the National Union of Teachers, released to the press at the end of February 1992, Prime Minister John Major accused the Labour Party of having introduced a secondary structure which fostered low standards and expectations:

> I am drawn to the view that the problem of low standards stems in large part from the nature of the comprehensive system which the Labour Party ushered in in the 1960s, and from the intellectual climate underpinning it that has tended to stress equality of *outcome* at the

> expense of equality of *opportunity* . . . The orthodoxy which has grown up around the comprehensive system has, frankly, been an orthodoxy of the Left: hostility to competition *between* schools and *between* pupils, and even in sport; hostility to all forms of testing; hostility to genuine parental choice; and a steady infiltration of such traditional curriculum subjects as history and English Literature by some questionable dogmas that fly in the face of common sense . . . I ask you not to doubt my sincerity and determination to reverse the failings of the comprehensive system and the cycle of low expectations and low standards which it has fostered. (reported in the *Guardian*, 28 February 1992)

Among the many distortions in this letter, the attempt to portray the comprehensive reform as a straightforwardly political issue is one for which no supporting evidence can be found in the various studies that have been undertaken of comprehensive reorganisation in this country (see, for example, Kerckhoff *et al.*, 1996). It was, after all, a Conservative authority, Leicestershire (governed by the representatives of traditional county families), that launched a bold plan in 1957 whereby a staged transition to comprehensive education could be facilitated by the use of existing, though transformed, schools in a two-tier (11–14, 14–18) system. Having gained power in October 1964, the Labour Government found that almost two-thirds of the secondary school population already lived in areas where the LEA was implementing or planning a comprehensive school policy – a point emphasised by Education Secretary Anthony Crosland in a speech delivered at the end of May 1965:

> The fact is that there has been a growing movement against the 11-plus examination and all that it implies. This movement has not been politically inspired or imposed from the centre. It has been a spontaneous growth at the grassroots of education, leading to a widespread conviction that separation is an offence against the child as well as a brake on social and economic progress . . . The whole notion of a selection test at this age belongs to the era when secondary education was a privilege of the few. (quoted in Kerckhoff *et al.*, 1996, p. 28)

The publication, two months later, of Circular 10/65 – requesting local education authorities, *if they had not already done so*, 'to prepare and submit to the Secretary of State plans for reorganising secondary education in their areas on comprehensive lines' – signified official recognition of the strength of the comprehensive movement throughout the country.

It is worth emphasising that in the 1960s and early 1970s local control by the Conservative Party was far from uniformly associated with the rejection of comprehensivisation; and that not all LEAs controlled by Labour were in favour of the comprehensive school. Indeed, many within the Labour Party were wary of abolishing the selective system because they viewed it as a relatively democratic mechanism for enabling a minority of working-class children to 'succeed' in an openly meritocratic society. Since Labour leaders had fought so hard to provide grammar-school places for the children of the working classes, these institutions – middle-class in ethos though many of them might be – were not to be surrendered lightly. Many middle-class parents, on the other hand, developed a remarkable attachment to their local comprehensive school – a fact Conservative politicians were to ignore at their peril when attempts were made to reintroduce 11-plus selection in certain key areas in the early 1980s.

THE COMPREHENSIVE PRINCIPLE UNDER THREAT

In the 1960s, an ideology of belief in the importance and inevitability of educational expansion was accompanied by growing dissatisfaction with the stratified system of schooling established in the 1940s as part of the early post-war consensus. The policy makers of the 1960s saw a direct and indisputable correlation between educational reform and general economic prosperity: a skilled and educated workforce, equipped by comprehensive schooling to meet the challenges of the technological revolution, would facilitate economic growth which would, in turn, constitute a firm basis for continuing educational expansion. As Maurice Plaskow has observed, for those who believed in a genuine extension of educational opportunity, it was surely 'the best of times':

> It is fashionable to deride the 1960s as culturally aberrant and wildly idealist. Healthy idealism may be preferable to entrenched ideology parading as pragmatism, which has been the chief characteristic of subsequent decades. Many of us who were active in education in the 1960s look back on a time of optimism, a spirit of shared concerns, and the beginnings of an articulation (in every sense) of an education system which would offer the greatest possible opportunities to everyone as an entitlement, not a privilege. (Plaskow, 1990, p. 90)

Yet this extraordinary spirit of optimism and hope was not to survive into the following decade which saw a reaction against the prevailing mood of the 1960s on a whole series of fronts, including education. This reaction was particularly marked after the economic crisis of the early 1970s that fundamentally altered the map of British politics and created the necessary conditions for the widespread dissemination of a whole new set of right-wing ideas.

The collapse of fixed exchange rates in 1971–72, followed by the quadrupling of the oil price in 1973, resulted in a generalised world recession which challenged many of the underlying assumptions of Keynesian social democracy. The post-war consensus had relied on increasing prosperity for such success as it might have had in creating a semblance of social unity; when that prosperity disintegrated, so too did consensus. The Conservative Party, led from February 1975 onwards by Margaret Thatcher, finally turned its back on what Sir Keith Joseph termed the 'middle ground' and opted instead for an updated version of the classical market liberalism of the nineteenth century. The Labour Party's leadership sought to appease the powerful capitalist establishment by distancing itself from many of its socialist supporters and showing due regard for the harsh realities created by the economic downturn.

As far as education was concerned, the Labour leadership's project was to emphasise the need to make more effective use of the money – roughly £6 billion a year – that the Government was spending on schools and, at the same time, to refute the Tory claim that Labour had no concern for standards or accountability. An important speech delivered by Prime Minister James Callaghan at Ruskin College, Oxford, in October 1976 signally failed to celebrate the achievements of the state education system. It was constructed against the background of widespread media denigration of the comprehensive school and the furore caused by the activities of a group of so-called 'progressive' teachers at the William Tyndale Junior and Infant Schools in London. While it refrained from directly attacking comprehensive education, it referred to public concern about the secondary system and, in particular, about its failure to fit youngsters 'to do a job of work'. In Callaghan's view, there was no virtue in encouraging comprehensive schools to produce 'socially well-adjusted members of society who are unemployed because they do not have the skills' (quoted in Chitty, 1989, p. 171).

Margaret Thatcher, on the other hand, was always quite open about her desire to undermine, and eventually destroy, the comprehensive system of secondary schooling. She bitterly resented the fact that, as Education Secretary in Edward Heath's Government from 1970 to 1974, she had been unable to overturn the prevailing orthodoxy that reorganisation was almost inevitable. It is often claimed that a lingering sense of shame about this helped to fuel her long-standing contempt for independent local authorities, DES officials, members of Her Majesty's Inspectorate and the educational 'establishment' as a whole. She herself gave credence to this view with a number of recollections to the effect that she had been up against entrenched conventional wisdom which had prevented her from 'saving' the grammar schools. In 1983 she told one interviewer:

> There was a great battle on. It was part of this equalisation rage at the time: that you mustn't select by ability. But, after all, I had come up by selection by ability. I had to fight it. I had a terrible time. (quoted in Young, 1989, p. 68)

And in May 1987, she confided to the editor of the *Daily Mail*:

> The universal comprehensive thing obviously started with Tony Crosland's 1965 Circular and all education authorities were asked to submit plans in which the schools were to go totally comprehensive. When I was the Minister for Education in the Heath Government . . . this great rollercoaster of an idea was moving, and I found it difficult, if not impossible, to stop. (interview in *Daily Mail*, 13 May 1987)

In Mrs Thatcher's view, most of the education correspondents of the time also had to accept some of the blame. In an interview with the Press Association News Agency at the beginning of May 1989, the Prime Minister said that she had never forgotten a terrible lunch with a group of gullible education correspondents in early 1970. Many of them had 'ridiculed' everything she stood for, and she added: 'They had simply swallowed hook, line and sinker compulsory comprehensive education. But they and I have lived to know that they were wrong' (reported in the *Independent*, 4 May 1989).

Yet the return of 11-plus selection did not prove to be the popular measure that many Conservative politicians imagined it to be. In the 1980s, there were concerted efforts to reintroduce or extend selective education in Berkshire, Wiltshire and the London Borough of Redbridge, and all met with severe local opposition and failed. Of particular significance here was the case of the West Midlands Borough of Solihull where Conservative councillors showed real misjudgement regarding community attachment to local schools. The plan to reintroduce selection was, in fact, defeated by the middle-class residents of areas like Dorridge and Balsall Common, who had no wish to see their popular local comprehensive schools turned into grammar schools selecting pupils from all parts of the borough (see Walford and Jones, 1986). Such defeats served to encourage Conservative Ministers to opt for rather more subtle policy initiatives aimed at establishing a wider variety of secondary schools and providing for greater parental choice.

THE 1988 EDUCATION ACT AND ITS AFTERMATH

It can be argued that the meretricious agenda of the 1988 Education Reform Act was in many ways a tribute to the remarkable resilience of the comprehensive ideal. And devices like opting out, open admission, city technology colleges and the introduction of 'local markets' can all be viewed as attempts to introduce selection by the back door.

Education Secretary Kenneth Baker was keen to emphasise the importance of differentiation and choice in an interview with Stuart Maclure which appeared at the beginning of April 1987:

> I want a much greater degree of variety and independence in the running of our schools. I do want to see a greater amount of variety and choice . . . What we have at present is seven per cent or so in the independent sector, probably going to rise to ten per cent; and on the other side, a huge continent: 93 per cent in the state-maintained sector. I'm responsible for that state sector. What I think is striking in the British education system is that there is *nothing in between* . . . Now the City Technology Colleges I've already announced are a sort of half-way house. I would like to see many more half-way houses, a greater choice, a greater variety. I think many parents would as well. (*Times Educational Supplement*, 3 April 1987)

For many Conservative politicians, the introduction of these 'half-way houses' meant the creation of new types of secondary school with selective implications without, at the same time, subjecting children to the strain of an unpopular competitive examination at the age of 11. Indeed, at a pre-election press conference held in May 1987, the Prime Minister herself argued that heads and governing bodies who opted out of local education authority control should be free to establish their own admissions policies and might even be able to charge fees (reported in the *Guardian*, 23 May 1987). Kenneth Baker responded by giving his own assurance that no proposal for 'a change of character' would be entertained within five years of a school acquiring grant-maintained status. This stipulation did not, however, appear in the 1987 Bill; and was in any case widely circumvented in all manner of covert ways. Research carried out by a team at the University of Leicester and published in 1993 revealed that around one-third of the first comprehensive schools to opt out of local control used some form of academic or social selection when over-subscribed. Methods for discriminating between applicants included: parent and/or pupil interviews, reports from the previous school and, in one case, written examinations (Bush *et al.*, 1993, p. 95), all of which seemed to support the view that the grant-maintained policy was leading to the development of a new two-tier system.

Yet despite fears that the new grant maintained schools would be in a strong position to undermine the comprehensive ideal, it soon became apparent in the early 1990s that opting out was not taking off all over the country, but was, in fact, popular only in local authorities that were either Conservative or low-spending – or both. According to a comprehensive analysis carried out by Local Schools Information (LSI) and published in February 1992, schools intending to opt out of local control were concentrated in just 12 of the 117 education authorities in England and Wales (see Chitty, 1992, p. 84). And this caused the Major Government of 1992–97 to investigate new ways of creating choice and diversity without resorting to overt selection.

THE NEW EMPHASIS ON SPECIALISATION

By the time John Patten became Education Secretary in April 1992, it was clear that specialisation had replaced selection as a guiding principle of Conservative policy.

The details of a new 'schools revolution', introducing 'the British version of the American "magnet school"', were spelled out as a front-page story at the beginning of May 1992:

> Education Secretary John Patten is looking at plans to turn some secondary schools into centres of excellence in key subject areas . . . This means that some schools will specialise in the academic subjects like languages, maths and science; some will be technically-based; and others might offer performing arts or sports as their new specialism . . . This move puts selection back on the education agenda – but it drives a final nail in the coffin of the campaign to bring back grammar schools and the 11-plus. (*Mail on Sunday*, 3 May 1992)

The Education Secretary himself argued in an article in the *New Statesman and Society* that socialists must now 'come to terms with the concept of specialisation':

> selection is not, and should not be, a great issue of the 1990s as it was in the 1960s. The S-word for all Socialists to come to terms with is, rather, 'specialisation'. The fact is that children excel at different things; it is foolish to ignore it, and some schools may wish specifically to cater for these differences. Specialisation, underpinned by the National Curriculum, will be the answer for some – though not all – children, driven by aptitude and interest, as much as by ability . . .
>
> It is clear that on to the foundation stone of the National Curriculum can be built the liberation of all the talents through greater specialisation in our schools. This could be specialisation *within* a large comprehensive, setting for this or that subject – by the pupils self-selecting, or being guided towards their choice by aptitude and commitment. Or it could be something that builds on to the schools – a leading edge in bilingually-taught technology, for example, or in music, or in the area where languages crucially meet business studies.
>
> Such schools are already emerging. They will, as much more than mere exotic educational boutiques, increasingly populate the educational landscape of Britain at the end of the century, a century that introduced universal education at its outset; then tried to grade children like vegetables; then tried to treat them . . . like identical vegetables; and which never ever gave them the equality of intellectual nourishment that is now being offered by the National Curriculum, encouraged by testing, audited by regular inspection. (Patten, 1992, pp. 20–1)

The White Paper *Choice and Diversity*, published in July 1992, vilified the comprehensive system for 'presupposing that children are all basically the same and that all local communities have essentially the same educational needs' (DfE, 1992, p. 3). It was the Government's view that 'the provision of education should be geared more to local circumstances and individual needs: hence a commitment to diversity in education' (pp. 3–4). The White Paper went on to argue that specialisation should not be confused with straightforward selection:

> The fact that a school is strong in a particular field may well increase the demand to attend, but it does not necessarily follow that selective entry criteria have to be imposed by the school. The selection that takes place is parent driven. The principle of open access remains. As demand to attend increases, so the school may simply require extra resources to cope with the range of talent available. (DfE, 1992, p. 10)

Somewhat confusingly, the White Paper announced plans to build on the work of the existing 15 city technology colleges by establishing *both* a network of maintained secondary schools with enhanced technology facilities, to be known as 'technology schools', *and* a network of schools established in partnership with business sponsors, to be known as 'technology colleges'. It was anticipated that schools seeking to become new technology colleges would want to do so as grant-maintained schools.

The key principle of providing a greater variety of schools, whatever the implications for selection inherent in such a project, was extended still further in a later Conservative White Paper, *Self-Government for Schools*, during Gillian Shephard's period as Education Secretary. The whole tone of the document was set in an early section headed 'Choice, Diversity and Specialisation' where we read that:

> Children have different abilities, aptitudes, interests and needs. These cannot all be fully met by a single type of school, at least at secondary level. The Government wants parents to be able to choose from a range of good schools of different types, matching what they want for their child with what a school offers. The choice should include schools which select by academic ability, so that the most able children have the chance to achieve the best of which they are capable . . . Independent schools, church schools and grammar schools have long offered choice for *some* parents. The Government has greatly expanded diversity through the Assisted Places Scheme, by setting up the 15 City Technology Colleges, and by giving all schools the opportunity to become grant maintained. It has also encouraged schools to specialise in particular subjects such as technology and languages. (DfEE, 1996b, pp. 2–3).

If the Conservatives had won the 1997 general election, grant-maintained schools would have been free to select up to 50 per cent of their intake by ability; technology and language colleges up to 30 per cent; and all remaining LEA schools up to 20 per cent.

THE CONSERVATIVE LEGACY

The Conservatives have bequeathed to New Labour a sharply divided system of secondary state schools. Any chance of creating a successful comprehensive structure subject to fair admissions rules will be seriously undermined by the continued existence of 163 grammar schools and 15 city technology colleges – together with a number of specialist schools and colleges that are able to 'select' pupils on the basis of their 'aptitude' for particular subjects such as technology, languages, sports or arts.

Yet despite the administrative confusion that Conservative policies have caused, Labour's response to most of the problems it has inherited has been decidedly ambivalent. On the question of grammar schools, for example, it has failed to give a clear lead, tending to regard their survival as an issue of minor significance. The policy for dealing with them outlined in the 1995 Labour policy document *Diversity and Excellence: A New Partnership for Schools*, was attacked by many, both inside and outside the Labour Party, for being disingenuous and unworkable. In the words of the document:

> Our opposition to academic selection at 11 has always been clear. But while we have never supported grammar schools in their exclusion of children by examination, change can come only through local agreement. Such change in the character of a school could only follow a clear demonstration of support from the parents affected by such decisions. (Labour Party, 1995, p. 11)

This document was published in June 1995. Then, at the Labour Party Conference on 4 October, Shadow Education Secretary David Blunkett told his audience: 'Read my lips. No selection by examination or interview.' That categorical assurance won the day for the Labour leadership; and the revolt, organised around demands for the remaining grammar schools to be incorporated into the comprehensive system, collapsed for the simple reason that its purpose seemed to have been achieved. However, it soon became clear that 'no selection' actually meant 'no *further* selection'; and the White Paper, *Excellence in Schools*, published in July 1997, repeats the 1995 formula by insisting that 'where grammar schools exist, local parents must have an interest in the decisions on whether their selective admissions arrangements should continue' (DfEE, 1997a, p. 72).

An already confused situation will be further exacerbated by Labour's proposal to phase out grant-maintained schools but at the same time introduce three new categories of school: 'community', 'aided' and 'foundation' – with only community schools subject to admissions procedures determined by the local authority. When this policy was first announced in *Diversity and Excellence*, it was widely criticised for encouraging the perpetuation of a divided system. For example, writing in the *Independent* on 22 June 1995, former Deputy Leader of the Labour Party, Roy Hattersley, argued that 'by building its policy around different classes of school, Labour is endorsing selection'. He made the obvious but important point that 'once a hierarchy of schools is established, those perceived as "best" always receive more than their proper share of resources'.

New Labour also seems quite happy to adopt the Conservative policy of 'selection by specialisation'. Schools are to be invited to 'play to their strengths' and recognise children's 'particular aptitudes'. Admissions policies can then include selection based on these 'perceived aptitudes'. According to *Excellence in Schools*: 'we will ensure that schools with a specialism will continue to be able to give priority to children who demonstrate the relevant aptitude, as long as that is not misused to select on the basis of general academic ability' (DfEE, 1997a, p. 71). What the White Paper fails to point out is that in a class-divided and competitive society specialisms are not equal: they rapidly become ranked in a hierarchy of status. It also makes the false assumption that children can actually be tested for particular talents rather than for general ability. As Professor Peter Mortimore argued in an article in *Education Guardian*, the body of research evidence suggests otherwise:

> Except in music and perhaps art, it does not seem possible to diagnose specific aptitudes for most school curriculum subjects. Instead, what emerges from such testing is a general ability to learn, which is often, but not always, associated with the various advantages of coming from a middle-class home. How can headteachers know if the 'aptitude' of a ten year old in German shows anything more than the parents' ability to pay for language lessons? (*Guardian*, 24 March 1998)

All of which helps to explain the alarm caused by clause 93 of the School Standards and Framework Bill, published on 4 December 1997, which states that a maintained school may 'make provision for the selection of pupils for admission to the school by reference to their aptitude for one or more prescribed subjects' where:

> a) the admission authority for the school is satisfied that the school has a specialism in the subject or subjects in question; and
> b) the proportion of selective admissions in any relevant age group does not exceed ten per cent.

THE COMPREHENSIVE IDEAL

Comprehensive education challenges the fallacy of fixed potential in education. At the secondary level, it stands for a genuine transformation of the system based on a belief in the educability of *all* children and in the futility of forcing them into outworn categories. As a practical reform, it involves dismantling structures that act as barriers to learning, while fashioning new practices that enable everyone, regardless of their circumstances, to have a full education.

Thirty years ago, the principle of fully comprehensive education was supported by about one-quarter of the population and opposed by about one-quarter – with all the rest undecided. By the beginning of 1996, the principle of everyone of secondary school age going to schools designed for all abilities was endorsed by 65 per cent of the population, while 27 per cent favoured a system where some schools catered for 'high ability' children and others for the 'remainder' – with only 8 per cent now unable to give a view (ICM poll, reported in the *Guardian*, 7 February 1996).

Yet, despite the popularity of the comprehensive ideal, New Labour politicians are extraordinarily defensive about the comprehensive system. There seems to be some curious understanding that the reforms of the 1950s and 1960s served to undermine the pursuit of 'excellence'. This marked reluctance to extol the virtues of comprehensive reorganisation is certainly evident in the 1997 White Paper:

> The demands for equality and increased opportunity in the 1950s and 1960s led to the introduction of comprehensive schools. All-in secondary schooling rightly became the normal pattern, but the search for equality of opportunity in some cases became a tendency to uniformity. The idea that all children had the same rights to develop their abilities led too easily to the doctrine that all had the same ability. The pursuit of excellence was too often equated with elitism. (DfEE, 1997a, p. 11).

Writing in the *Independent on Sunday* in January 1995, Professor Ben Pimlott argued that New Labour should be proud to promote the cause of the comprehensive school:

> There are exciting possibilities here. Education is a key concern of Tony Blair, as of every parent in the country: the policy aim of turning Britain's comprehensives into the best in Europe, after 16 years of criminal neglect, would create excitement throughout our cities; but only if New Labour offered the resources to make it all credible. (*Independent on Sunday*, 8 January 1995)

But his words have gone unheeded as Labour politicians have preferred to believe that many comprehensive schools are performing badly and therefore need 'modernising'. Nowhere is there a clear realisation that the divided system itself militates against comprehensive success.

The authors of the 1997 White Paper are clearly proud of the oft-repeated 'standards not structures' mantra – a banal catchphrase which first saw the light of day in *The Blair Revolution: Can New Labour Deliver?*, co-authored by Peter Mandelson and Roger Liddle and published in 1996. We are told that the preoccupation with structure has absorbed a great deal of energy to little effect, although it is not made clear exactly what the word 'structure' means in this context. If it refers to the structure of the education system as a whole, one is tempted to ask what sort of national framework we would now have if large numbers of parents, teachers, local education authorities and politicians had not cared about 'structure' in the 1950s and 1960s and campaigned vigorously for a comprehensive system of secondary schooling. If it refers to the 'structure' of individual schools (which, in any case, cannot be viewed in isolation from the system as a whole), then we are being asked to consider a false dichotomy. Standards and structures are interrelated and can be understood only in relation to each other. As Caroline Benn and I discovered, a comprehensive school which is, in reality, a secondary modern in a still selective local system with inadequate resources to perform a wide variety of tasks is less likely to achieve 'excellent' results of the kind measured by Ofsted than will another school in the same area occupying a safe and privileged position in the local hierarchy of schools (Benn and Chitty, 1996).

Only when the Labour Government understands the importance of creating a single unified system of fully comprehensive secondary schools under local democratic control and without selective enclaves, will the country have an education system of which we can truly be proud. The divisions inherited from 18 years of Conservative rule have to be viewed as serious obstacles to the provision of a high-quality education for *all* pupils.

4

CHANGING PRESSURES IN THE SECONDARY SCHOOL

PETER DOWNES

Many of the pressures for change which have already been mentioned in this volume in connection with primary schools are similar to those for the secondary sector. Indeed, the concept of 'pressure' has affected all levels of the education service. From pre-school right through to university, teachers and administrators have experienced significant changes which have made the challenges of daily work more complex and increased levels of professional stress. Whether it has decreased the enjoyment and satisfaction of being 'in education' is a moot point. Although many complain about what has happened over the past 20 years, there are clearly others for whom the greater freedom and enhanced autonomy have brought personal fulfilment.

It is therefore essential not to view everything that has happened during the Conservative period of office in a negative light. Perhaps changes were necessary – we had become too comfortable, too self-contained, too lethargic in our response to the changing demands of society. It could be argued that, in some parts of the country, the local councillors wielded too much power and that political ideology produced a school system which was inefficient, gave priority to social objectives rather than educational ones and failed to produce the equality of opportunity on which it was allegedly based.

The changes of the Conservative era affected secondary schools more immediately than primary because the main principles of Conservative educational policy – choice and diversity – could change the structure more easily and more rapidly at secondary level. Given that there are six times as many primary schools as secondary schools, structural change at secondary level (the introduction of grant-maintained schools, city technology colleges and specialist schools) could make an impact more rapidly. Older children could be expected to travel further to school and thereby exercise choice. The established public examinations at 16 and 18 allowed a more immediate focus on achievement.

The changes outlined in the opening chapter have transformed the life of the secondary school headteacher since 1979. While it is true that life has changed in many ways for the classroom teacher, the change in the work of the headteacher has been dramatic. The classroom teacher of the late 1990s still grapples, as teachers always have done, with classroom management, with making lessons interesting, with maintaining discipline, with preparing and marking. What classroom teachers now do is laid down with much greater specificity; their work is more closely monitored and they are more likely to be criticised than their predecessors; they need a wider range of technological skills; and the work is undoubtedly more demanding but it is still essentially the same as it was before the Thatcher Revolution.

The role of the headteacher, on the other hand, has changed more extensively. Heads are now expected to have a range of knowledge and skills unheard of 20 years ago. In those far-off days, it was sufficient to have been a 'good teacher' (a creature undefined but intuitively perceived by the transmitted wisdom of the profession), then a 'successful Head of Department' (although once again the criteria for success were never laid down). Deputy headship required versatility (often in a range of routine but time-consuming tasks), hard work, good public-speaking skills and the capacity to manage people happily. Those with the ambition to proceed further, and blessed with good interviewing technique and with a spark of vision or originality, made it to headship. In the past decade, heads have had to learn about financial management, legal and personnel issues; they have had to become public relations experts and negotiators with industry and government agencies. They have had to acquire an understanding of school maintenance, if not the physical skills to carry it out (although even that is not unknown). They have had to acquire information technology skills at a relatively late stage in their lives and they now have to be proficient in data analysis and research methodology.

From the head's perspective, the focal points of pressure are greater accountability and increased management responsibility because of local management of schools (LMS).

GREATER ACCOUNTABILITY

Looking back to the pre-1980 period, we may find it quite remarkable that heads and teachers were allowed to get on with their jobs with little interference from non-professionals. There was closer oversight from the LEA but this varied from place to place. In some LEAs, the councillors took a close personal interest in the detail of what went on in schools and sought to stamp their ideology on them. In many other cases, LEA officers were left to get on with their job and the rapport between them and the headteachers was one of mutual professional recognition and positive partnership. Heads moved into the LEA advisory service, either on secondment or permanently, and there was a sense of being part of a team, more or less effectively led by the Chief Education Officer, who enjoyed the freedom to make his or her own mark on the LEA. Looking back, it all seems cosy, comfortable and professionally insulated.

The head and the teaching staff were free to devise the curriculum structure and were notionally free to teach what they wanted. There was, of course, an implicit national curriculum dictated by public expectation that everybody would at least do English and mathematics, together with a range of options which could be tailored to meet the needs of pupils. The detail of the teaching was strongly influenced by the examination boards, but there were so many syllabuses and boards to choose from that most teachers could select whatever suited them. Most teaching materials presented a subject in its 'pure' form, that is, geography as the author construed it, not geography for a specific syllabus. Within these overall constraints, heads and teachers were remarkably free.

It is true that schools had governing bodies but these met not more than once a term and there were usually no sub-committees, except for some special purpose, such as a new building programme. Some of the more diligent governors showed an interest in the detail of what was happening and some visited during the school day but, for the most part, the governors were at arm's length, receiving reports from the head (who thereby effectively controlled the agenda) and fulfilling what now, from the perspective of hindsight, looks like a largely symbolic and ceremonial role.

Parents, particularly in the secondary sector, were not positively encouraged to become involved in the school other than as fund-raisers. The whole tone of the pre-1980 period was that the school knew best and the job of the parent was to make children conform to what the school expected. Pupils had very little say in what went on in school and in the educational programme. They were the recipients of whatever the school, benign and caring, thought was best for them. In some enlightened schools, pupils were invited to have their say in elected school councils, but the level of discussion rarely got above complaints about school dinners and the quality of the toilet paper.

There was little pressure from the wider public because they knew very little about what went on within a school. There would be occasional major scandals and crises, and the local press would report on school plays and concerts, trips and star pupils, but it was all quite comfortable for the teaching profession in general and for heads in particular, provided they managed to avoid a disaster.

The sequence of Education Acts through the 1980s burst open the world of the school in all these domains and it is this increased pressure to be accountable on many fronts which has contributed to the raising of standards, more than the structural or managerial changes of LMS. The governors, restructured to have a wider representation of parents and teachers as well as the traditional local worthies, have seen an enormous increase in their responsibilities and workload. The termly meeting of the full governing body has been increased to two in many schools, such is the volume of work, and sub-committees have burgeoned as every aspect of the school's work has come under scrutiny. Although there are still some heads who try to hang on to the notion of the governing body as a rubber-stamp, such is the insight, expertise and dedication of most governors that they have become a powerful factor for school improvement. Parent governors in particular take themselves and their work very seriously.

The LEA's role as monitor and guardian of standards, whatever they were, has been taken over by Ofsted, one of the most rigorous and public school inspection systems anywhere in the world. The meeting with parents without the head there, the detailed scrutiny of all aspects of the work of the school, the publication of the report, the requirement for an action plan – all these have put the public spotlight on the work of the school in general and the head in particular. It is little wonder that the early retirement of heads has become the norm rather than the exception in the past few years. Where our predecessors could potter happily on to 65, the pressure of headship today is so great that people are 'burning out' at 55 or younger. One of the last acts of the Conservative Government, the closing down of the loophole of early retirement, served to highlight the crisis in school leadership. It may well be that this development, prompted initially by the need to keep the Teachers Pension Agency within some kind of budgetary control, will turn out to be the catalyst for a changing concept of headship. To be a head was to reach the pinnacle of the profession and was the basis for the best pension. Perhaps headship will become a pinnacle which is reached earlier in life and then left before the job becomes burdensome, a transformation which the pension system will need to recognise.

Before 1980, most headteachers were conscious of the need to keep the parents happy. Every head liked to think that parents had a good opinion of the school. The new pressure from parents has been in the significant change in their participation in the educational process. In addition to greater representation on governing bodies and all their statutory opportunities to question the school, parents have above all been cast in the role of customers. Open enrolment and the marketplace philosophy were based on the assumption that parents would shop around for the 'best school'. In many parts of the country, especially those areas where transport allows choice, parents have become a constituency which heads simply cannot ignore. Heads have learned what the world of business means by 'the customer is always right'. The amount of time given to parents by heads and deputies, both as individuals and as a collective group, has increased phenomenally in recent years. Handling complaints, following up problems and negotiating outcomes to relationship crises have all become major activities for senior staff. 'The school knows best' simply will not do any more.

As for the press and general public, the awareness of educational issues has risen dramatically. Now, scarcely a day passes without an article in the national newspapers about schools. Much of the discussion is at a level of pedagogical detail unheard of until this decade. Exactly how are children being taught to read? Should they be taught in whole classes or in groups? Exactly what messages are being put across through the National Curriculum? Are standards falling because more young people are achieving higher grades or does that mean that standards are rising? The league tables of examination results, fallible and professionally rubbished as they are, are scrutinised by the public who now have come to expect an ever increasing level of technical detail. The changes proposed by the new Government – value-added league tables and three-year trends – will only increase the pressure on schools because they will reveal the truth more fully than was done in the past.

Heads' opinions on this massive increase in accountability are by no means uniform. Some resent the amount of time which they have to put into public relations, time which they think could be better spent in making a more direct educational input to school. Some heads have become paranoiac about litigious parents and have become so cautious about what might go wrong that they are reluctant to sanction activities which might involve any kind of risk. Those hostile to these developments argue that the combination of central control of the curriculum linked with detailed public scrutiny have simply made the job of headship impossible to fulfil with satisfaction.

The contrary view is that the opening up of schools to public interest is a welcome and long overdue development. As employees funded by the public purse, heads and teachers must recognise that they can no longer just get on with the job regardless of public pressure. The fierce public debate surrounding education is to be welcomed if it increases public readiness for greater investment. What the public needs to recognise is that the demands on heads have increased to the point where it will become physically impossible to meet them if resources continue to be cut back. Heads can do what the Government, Ofsted, parents, governors, public and pupils demand of them, but not without a strong senior management team and substantial administrative support.

LOCAL MANAGEMENT OF SCHOOLS

The second area of pressure for secondary school heads came from the implementation of local management of schools (LMS), which did not, however, come as a bolt from the blue. Earlier versions, giving heads greater control over the financial aspect of management, had been tried out in various parts of the country (Inner London, Solihull and Cambridgeshire, for example) but the full impact of the reforms came in the 1988 version of LMS. The responsibility for managing large sums of public money, with the freedom to appoint more or fewer staff, spend more or less on books and equipment, employ more or fewer non-teaching staff, was welcomed by the vast majority of heads, notwithstanding their lack of preparation for such a change in their role. The introduction of LMS went more smoothly in the secondary sector than in primary schools where the lack of support staff left the head exposed, sometimes to his or her own inadequacies.

Three features of LMS were attractive and remain so:

- the flexibility to apply resources according to the particular needs of the individual establishment. Although all schools perform a broadly similar task, the circumstances of each institution are so different that the imaginative head could apply the resources more effectively, no longer being hidebound by externally determined staffing limits, allocations for capitation and LEA maintenance budgets;
- the incentive to be cost-effective meant that heads were always seeking ways of delivering good education less expensively because the money saved could be recycled into providing other benefits for the school;

- the sense of autonomy, the feeling of really being 'in charge' lifted the morale of heads in the early days of LMS.

After the Education Reform Act in 1988, the mood of many heads was one of excitement and challenge. They were finding out about many aspects of the costing of education of which they had previously been ignorant. Previously most heads would not have known how much it cost to run the school but now they knew it in great detail. Some took a particular delight in finding cheaper ways of buying electricity, in obtaining equipment more cheaply or bargaining with local tradesmen. Meetings of heads were dominated by a scrutiny of the mechanics of accountancy and by the exchange of tips for better value for money. Certainly, it brought increased pressure but it was not unwelcome.

The disadvantages and harmful pressures became apparent more gradually. Firstly, LMS soaked up time from the head's daily schedule. Many classroom teachers resented the fact that heads became obsessed with finance and appeared to stop thinking about the true educational purpose of the school. Indeed, rank-and-file teachers viewed the whole thrust of LMS with considerable suspicion: more experienced and therefore more expensive teachers felt threatened; heads of 'expensive' departments, such as design and technology or science, had to argue even harder for their traditional slice of the cake when it came to the distribution of 'capitation'.

The second disadvantage of LMS from the head's point of view was that, although it may have been enjoyable moving money between budget headings in times of relative stability of funding and of pupil numbers, this was difficult when the school roll and funding declined. Then the head was perceived as the person who had to make the unpopular decisions and was thus more exposed to criticism. Heads who tried to involve staff in taking greater responsibility for financial decisions within the school, for example by devolving more autonomy to departmental cost-centre level, found high levels of resistance. This was partly because heads of department were so highly stretched introducing the new GCSE exam and then the National Curriculum that they did not have the mental capacity for a further set of responsibilities. More fundamentally, resistance came from heads of department sharp enough to realise that, the smaller the size of the cost centre, the more difficult and personal the decisions become. The head of department, faced with a shrinking budget, would at least be able to 'blame it on the head', just as the head had previously blamed it on the LEA.

The third and most serious difficulty caused for heads by LMS was an essential part of the Conservative marketplace philosophy. The bulk of the funding for the school was directly related to the number of pupils on the roll. The legislation required that 80 per cent of funding should be distributed according to a formula driven by the number of pupils, weighted by the age of the pupil. The ugly acronym AWPU (Age-Weighted Pupil Unit) became part of the everyday jargon of heads who had to try to predict their AWPU score for the next five years in order to plan for reduction or expansion. Falling rolls, whether by demographic change over which heads had no control, or by unpopularity, for which they may have had some responsibility, were extremely difficult to manage. This was because rolls did not fall in neat multiples of class size. A school used to taking an intake of 180 taught in six classes of 30 might find itself with a cohort of 160, still needing to be taught in six groups, yet losing the funding for 20 pupils, sufficient to cause the loss of a member of the teaching staff but with the same amount of teaching to be provided. This process continuing over a number of years posed severe difficulties. Even the protection of smaller schools by a special lump sum scarcely alleviated the problem.

The effect of number-driven funding was to cause heads to become more conscious of the need to 'market' the school. Many found the commercial connotations of marketing hard to stomach in the liberal profession of headship (Bridges and McLaughlin, 1994, pp. 54–64). Most felt that they had come into teaching as a public service, not in order to market their own school to the disadvantage of neighbouring schools. Since children cannot be procreated ready-made at the age of 11-plus, every extra pupil recruited by one school meant one fewer elsewhere. There was a sudden growth in the production of glossy brochures. Some heads went on recruiting campaigns, others advertised outside their catchment area. Indeed, the very notion of catchment area had all but disappeared under the pressure of 'open enrolment'. In the larger cities, the free market ruled and pupils could take transport, or be transported, to what were perceived to be the better schools. The present Prime Minister, when leader of the Opposition, famously exercised that option.

Many heads were extremely uncomfortable to see the law of the marketplace widening the gap between the more successful and the less successful schools, particularly as 'success' often depended on factors outside the control of the head or the staff. The publication of examination results in league-table form was another piece in the jigsaw of the marketplace philosophy. Heads were torn between looking after their own school, in which they now had an enhanced sense of autonomy and pride, and protecting the overall equity of the education system.

Others relished the new opportunities to be entrepreneurial and aggressively free-market. The grant-maintained (GM) option, sweetened by financial incentives, was taken up for a variety of reasons: some heads were unashamedly competitive (including a few who engineered significant pay rises for themselves in the process) and relished the excitement of the even greater freedom offered by GM status; others acquired GM status to avoid closure, or to save the sixth form, or to open a sixth form which the LEA had denied them; others took the GM route to escape from the administrative incompetence or political interference of their former LEA.

It has been argued that GM status was a logical extension of LMS and that there was no significant difference of principle between the two. The opposing view is that the advantages of GM schools, which increased as they were given greater freedom to select pupils, take up private finance initiatives, apply for specialist school status and benefit from higher levels of capital funding, were deleterious to a coherent and cohesive educational system across the country. In many parts of the country the legacy of GM is division and bitterness which the new post-1998 structures will not easily overcome. Fortunately, that is not the case everywhere; in some areas the previous partnership, higher professional ethos and straightforward camaraderie have kept LM and GM heads working together so that the recreation of a loosely administered light-touch LEA will not cause major problems.

THE FUTURE PROSPECTS FOR SECONDARY SCHOOLS

As the opening chapter of this book made clear, the manifesto commitments and the early actions of the Labour Government have shown modified continuity with the previous regime rather than wholesale rejection of it. The pressures will not be removed and there will be no return to the educational world of the 1970s.

Within the curriculum, there may be some easing of pressure in terms of content but not in terms of standards. Key stage 4 will become more flexible to meet the widely differing needs of individual pupils. The biggest changes are needed in post-16 education, where the greater breadth of a baccalaureate system would better equip young people for the world of the future. This issue is dealt with more fully in Chapter 5. As far as the head is concerned, the National Curriculum review could mean a return to the pedagogic and curriculum leadership role which has been underplayed in recent years.

The pressure of accountability will be intensified as the changes to the league tables, showing value-added as well as, or instead of, raw results, will more cruelly expose the strengths and weaknesses of different schools. The rigour of inspection, the more rapid dismissal of incompetent teachers, more immediate intervention by LEAs where schools are deemed to be failing – all this will intensify pressure on headteachers. The world of school leadership is not going to become any easier.

The principles of LMS are to be maintained and extended under devolved funding (DF). The new structure will be a compromise between LMS and GM status, giving schools greater management freedom with a higher percentage of the budget, but giving them less control over admissions. In this way, it might be possible to make better use of school buildings, avoiding wasteful duplication, empty spaces in some schools with overcrowding in others. The LEA, as defined in the code of practice for devolved funding to schools, will have the role of banker and enabler, providing those services which schools need to purchase collectively, but being above all a monitor of quality and a coordinator of admissions. The LEA will provide only what schools individually cannot offer, for example a well-resourced service for children with special needs, and other inter-school services such as transport. What it is not expected to do is to revert to the political interference in the details of school life which brought local government into such disrepute in the 1970s and which fuelled many of the Conservative reforms. Whether this will happen in practice is one of the unanswered questions for the future. It could be that the tension between 'Old Labour' in the LEAs and 'New Labour' in Westminster will be the political battleground of the new era.

A new pressure on secondary heads is whether to advise their governors to seek specialist status. The concept of schools specialising in technology, languages, sport or the arts appears not only to be accepted by the new Government but is to be developed. Given the strong financial incentive of £200,000 in capital funding (half from sponsors and half from central government) and £100,000 per year in revenue funding for three years, with a possible extension to six, it is going to be more difficult for idealistic heads to adhere to egalitarian principles. Commitment to being head of a high-quality generalist school, aiming for good all-round provision and offering the widest possible range of opportunities to all young people, will be hard to sustain under financial pressure.

The pressure of accountability shows no sign of decreasing. Chapter 11 shows how parents will be playing a greater role. As members of LEA Education Committees, they will be elected by a constituency to whom they will report back and from whom they will take guidance, if not be directly mandated. There seem to be two ways forward: either there will have to be a more fully developed parents' council in each school, with an LEA parents' council and a national parents' council (rather along the lines of the French model); or, the parent governors will have to meet as a group and find more direct ways than are presently available of canvassing parental opinion. Whichever pattern is chosen, it looks as though parental involvement in educational issues (as distinct from the fund-raising and social PTA [Parent–Teacher Association] role) on a more regular basis than the once-a-year annual meeting and the once-in-every-six-years Ofsted meeting will take up an increasing amount of headteacher time.

A new area of pressure for secondary heads will come from pupils and students who will be taking much greater personal responsibility for their own learning and who will develop a much fuller role in the life of the school. If we are to develop citizenship in schools as part of the more open society to which the Government is committed, it must not only be presented as a classroom subject but embodied in the structure of the school. Elected pupil councils, participation in the decision-making process and pupil evaluation of teachers could well be on the agenda. Such a development, which many believe to be educationally and democratically desirable, will test the diplomacy and ingenuity of heads to the full.

It is already clear that the new Government intends to improve schools through the increased competence of the teaching profession, with a strengthened structure of training and accreditation. Continuing professional development (CPD) will chart the career progression of the new generation of teachers. Looking back on the battles surrounding the introduction of teacher appraisal in the late 1980s, it is remarkable how rapidly the labelling and classification of teachers has progressed. The teacher appraisal scheme has been so gentle as to have had very little effect. Now we have the seven-point Ofsted scale for classroom performance and each stage of a teaching career – expert teacher, advanced skills teacher, subject leader, headteacher – is to be assessed according to a centralised framework. The Teacher Training Agency's long list of skills, attributes, knowledge and understanding is daunting: it is a far cry from the haphazard career development of most of the older generation of heads. This more thorough and systematic approach to CPD is going to change the role of the head, who will have to take a much closer interest in the career development of his or her staff. There may even be a subversive role for heads to counter the potential TTA cloning process which risks taking the individuality out of teaching. It will be essential for heads to cherish the idiosyncratic and colourful characters who can make the learning process come alive and bring academic sparkle into the lives of young people.

The greatest source of concern in relation to future pressures on secondary schools is finance. It is a fashionable political cliché that 'you can't solve problems by throwing money at them' and it is true that much improvement can be achieved by better administration, by enhancing teaching skills and by visionary management. Problems arise when you try to implement an ambitious programme in order to raise standards in a period of financial difficulty. Compared with many other European countries, education in the UK has never been generously funded, but since 1993 there has been a decline in real terms of about 6 per cent. The impact of this reduction has been felt differentially across the country because of the vagaries of the antiquated system for the distribution of educational funding. One of the unforeseen spin-offs of LMS has been the increased awareness by heads and governors of the arcane and inequitable method of funding schools in different parts of the country. Many people now recognise the absurdity of a situation in which schools have to follow a centralised curriculum, be judged by a central inspection system, pay teachers according to a nationally determined pay scale and meet centrally set targets and yet are funded in a way that produces huge discrepancies between schools in very similar socio-economic circumstances but which happen to be located in different LEAs.

There is an urgent need for a radical reform of the national funding mechanism and for a real-terms increase in the level of funding in schools. Ideally, the bulk of the extra funding should be directed at younger pupils to give them a firmer foundation but this cannot be done at the expense of the secondary sector as in recent years. Many secondary schools are functioning close to the point of collapse, almost unable to offer full-time schooling to all their pupils. The new Government's commitment to maintaining public spending at the level specified by the outgoing Government could undermine its aspirations for massive school improvement. It is estimated that it would cost about an extra £2 billion to restore revenue expenditure to an adequate level in schools (provided the distribution mechanism, and particularly the area cost adjustment, were reformed).

It remains to be seen if the Government's hints at increased capital expenditure materialise. It would cost £3.5 billion to clear the backlog of repairs to schools, many of which were built with flat roofs in the 1960s and 1970s and are now coming to the end of their anticipated lifespan. Although it is always possible to cite examples of excellent teaching in poor conditions, the fact remains that, for pupils in school, as for adults at work, the quality of the environment and the equipment make an enormous difference to morale, attitude and performance.

In difficult financial times, it is the head who is at the focal point of the tensions. It is he or she who has to guide governors into making the most difficult choices, between teachers and books, between larger classes or undecorated rooms. The original attractions of LMS – flexibility and autonomy – lose their appeal to heads when they face successive years of losing teaching staff, of running jumble sales to buy library books, or of reducing the very non-teaching staff whose value has been one of the great discoveries of the last decade.

Caught in the pincer movement of higher expectations from Government and fewer resources with which to meet those expectations, secondary heads are being put in an impossible position. The dilemma they face can be resolved only by a national decision that investment in education is such a priority that adequate public funding has to be found, if necessary out of increased direct taxation. Until this nettle is grasped, the attempts by the new Government to build on the educational successes and innovations of the last one will be fruitless and the pressures on secondary schools will be destructive.

5

TOWARDS RATIONALISATION? THE 14–19 CURRICULUM

JOHN DUNFORD

In 1982, I attended a regional meeting of the Secondary Heads Association (SHA) at which the president, Dr Peter Andrews, reflected on the rapid changes occurring in the school curriculum. He contrasted this with the recollection of a former colleague who had taught chemistry for 11 years with just one small alteration in the examination syllabus during that time. But the speed of change accelerated and, in the 16 years after 1982, teachers complained bitterly about the lack of stability in the curriculum and about the measures which were forced on them, often seemingly with little rationale other than political convenience.

Yet, in spite of all the changes, the post-16 curriculum in many schools in 1999 looks much the same as it did in 1979, and not very different from that in 1959. General Certificate of Education (GCE) Advanced levels predominate and breadth is often provided by a dash of general studies and some physical education. Many schools have introduced vocational qualifications alongside Advanced ('A') levels, but these are normally taught as separate courses. The lack of a coherent structure for 16–19 qualifications, which has been a feature of the past 20 years, remains, continuing to frustrate school curriculum planners at the end of the twentieth century.

If the 14–19 curriculum is taken as a whole, then the picture is even more fragmented. Indeed, the divisions between pre-16 and post-16 are sharper than they were in 1979. Key stage 4, as the two-year period from age 14 to 16 has become known in National Curriculum-speak, has undergone many changes, and it is now more disjoint from the post-16 curriculum.

CULTURAL FACTORS

Sally Tomlinson has drawn attention to the cultural factors operating on the 14–19 curriculum between the general elections of 1979 and 1997:

> Until the 1970s, even into the 1980s, the division between those who were academically successful and moved into higher education and professional jobs, and those who entered vocational training or unskilled employment at 16, still made economic sense. Only a minority of young people were considered to need professional, scientific, technological and executive expertise. All this is now changing. (Tomlinson, 1997, p. 109)

However, as Tomlinson goes on to point out:

> Education 14–19 is not yet a cohesive system for the majority. It is fragmented in institutional, curricula, assessment and organizational terms. It is still dogged by a leaving age at 16, by early selection, by an academic-vocational divide, and by competing qualifications offered by organisations with strong vested interests. The academic route is still highly specialized and narrow and the vocational route is incoherent and confused. (Tomlinson, 1997)

In 1979, 88 per cent of secondary school pupils were being educated in comprehensive schools; by 1997 this had risen to over 90 per cent. Yet the curriculum remains divided between academic sheep, vocational goats and those who are rejecting what is offered on both tracks. The challenge for the Labour Government is not to find a vocational alternative into which those who are rejecting the present systems can be placed, but to plan a comprehensive curriculum for the start of the twenty-first century, reflecting the needs and aspirations of young people for a less stratified and fairer society and equipping them for the more flexible employment market towards which Britain has already begun to move.

TOWARDS COHERENCE

In 1979, the headteacher had considerable control over the curriculum which was taught to young people from the age of 14. True, GCE Ordinary and Advanced level syllabuses were laid down by the examination boards, but the boards offered several syllabuses in each subject and it was always possible to change from one board to another. In the Certificate of Secondary Education (CSE), there was greater flexibility. Although schools used their own regional CSE board and there was not much choice between the CSE Mode 1 syllabuses (laid down by the CSE boards), Mode 3 offered schools the opportunity to design their own syllabuses. Equally important, schools were able to devise their own plans for the assessment of Mode 3 candidates. Many students who would not have achieved grade C at Ordinary level obtained the equivalent grade one CSE pass and built their portfolio of qualifications with a combination of Ordinary levels and CSE grade ones.

The Schools Council, which had been established in 1964 as an independent body with a majority of teacher members, lasted until 1982, when it was abolished by the Secretary of State, Sir Keith Joseph. It was surprising that it had not been abolished in the early 1970s when Margaret Thatcher was Secretary of State, because the Schools Council represented all that she detested about the world of education. Its governing body was determined to protect teachers' professional autonomy and its projects were often progressive and child centred. It had no control, only influence, and its most important missionaries were the staff inspectors in HMI, who, in direct proportion to their enthusiasm for individual Schools Council projects, encouraged schools to introduce them into the curriculum. Headteachers and heads of subject departments in secondary schools either accepted or rejected this advice. It was a cafeteria approach to school curriculum planning. Not only were Schools Council projects disseminated arbitrarily around the country's schools, but the evaluation of the projects was largely non-existent.

On abolishing the Council, Joseph established two bodies, the Schools Examination Council (SEC) and the Schools Curriculum Development Council (SCDC). In doing this, he made two errors which were perpetuated for more than ten years and which dogged the introduction of the National Curriculum. It was a mistake to have separate bodies for curriculum and assessment, an error which was not corrected until the School Curriculum and Assessment Authority (SCAA) was formed in 1993 from the National Curriculum Council (NCC) and the School Examinations and Assessment Council (SEAC), which had succeeded SEC and SCDC in 1988. The second important error was to reduce the membership of professional educators on these bodies and to fill the places with industrialists and political appointees. There were good reasons for the former to be represented, but the right-wing ideologues who sat on all these quangos did immense damage, not only to the process of curriculum development but to the credibility of the bodies on which they sat. They never succeeded in gaining the confidence of those engaged in the daily job of teaching children.

BREADTH AND BALANCE

In 1976, Prime Minister James Callaghan made a widely reported speech, in which he put forward the case for a stronger public interest in education. It was very rare for a Prime Minister to speak about education and the impact of his message was considerable. He expressed concern about the poor preparation of young people as future employees and he argued for a core curriculum of basic knowledge. Although the so-called 'Great Debate' on education which followed his speech was neither great nor a debate, the seeds of discontent had been sown and, by the time that the Conservative Government assumed office in 1979, the inspectorate had produced their seminal survey on secondary education, providing evidence for some of Callaghan's assertions on curriculum in the later years of compulsory education (DES, 1979, 13–43). Option schemes for 14 and 15 year olds, the survey found, were too wide and lacked coherence.

Meanwhile, the move towards a core curriculum from age 5 to 16 was gathering pace with the publication by HMI of three Red Books, in which they described an entitlement curriculum in terms of eight areas of experience – aesthetic and creative, ethical, linguistic, mathematical, physical, scientific, social and political, and spiritual. A ninth area – technological – was subsequently added to the list (DES, 1977; DES, 1981a; DES, 1983a).

During this period the DES published two documents on the school curriculum which clearly illustrated the growing interest of central government in what was taking place in school classrooms (DES, 1980a; DES, 1981b). In addition, Circulars 6/81 and 8/83 asked local education authorities to review their curriculum policies and to report to the Government on the curriculum in their schools. This came as something of a shock to LEAs, which had hitherto left the curriculum in the hands of headteachers.

At the North of England Conference in 1984, Sir Keith Joseph made a significant speech in which he proposed that the curriculum for all pupils should be broad and balanced up to the age of 16 and that it should be more closely related to life outside school, preparing young people better for working life. He laid down minimum levels of attainment to be achieved by 80 to 90 per cent of pupils by the age of 16 and proposed that examinations at 16 should be criterion referenced, rather than norm referenced, so that levels of attainment could be assessed by grade-related criteria. It was one of the greatest educational disappointments of the 1980s that it proved impossible to introduce criterion-referenced assessment. These themes were reinforced in an important Government White Paper, *Better Schools* (DES, 1985, p. 22).

The Senior Chief Inspector, Eric Bolton, was putting forward similar views, arguing that option schemes in the last two years of compulsory education should be replaced by a common curriculum of eight or nine subjects. HMI publications, particularly the *Curriculum Matters* series, reinforced this line of argument. The Schools Curriculum Development Council was a weak body and it was the DES and HMI which were clearly leading the curriculum debate at this time. In fact, most secondary schools still had extensive option systems for 14 and 15 year olds. Typically, the core curriculum comprised English, mathematics, physical education, careers and personal and social education, with pupils being given a choice of six subjects from a wide menu. In most schools, the choice was constrained so that all pupils did at least one science subject. Some schools also insisted that pupils studied at least one humanities subject, one subject in technology or the arts, and one modern foreign language, but this was by no means universal. Other schools structured their curriculum so that all pupils of this age studied integrated science, integrated humanities and an expressive arts course, but breadth and balance in the curriculum were in short supply for most young people.

GENERAL CERTIFICATE OF SECONDARY EDUCATION (GCSE)

For many years there had been discussions about a common examination at 16-plus to replace GCE and CSE, a two-tier system which reflected an earlier age of grammar and secondary modern schools. As Secretary of State for Education in the Labour Government in 1976, Shirley Williams had perhaps the best chance to introduce an examination system fit for a country in which almost all pupils were educated in comprehensive schools, but she wasted the opportunity. Ironically, it fell to Sir Keith Joseph, hardly the most egalitarian of Ministers, to announce the introduction of the GCSE. The first GCSE courses began in September 1986 and the first examinations were held in 1988. The teachers' associations complained strongly about the time-scale for the introduction of the new courses which, they considered, was at least one year too short. However, the Government was determined to press ahead and a 'cascade' model of in-service training was used, with local authority advisers and inspectors transmitting the information on the new syllabuses and assessment methods to the teachers. For the first and only time in the recent history of education, assessment was made to fit the curriculum, instead of the other way round. The final percentage GCSE mark was calculated from a combination of coursework, projects and terminal examinations, in proportions appropriate for each syllabus. Some courses were assessed only by terminal examinations; others were assessed entirely through coursework; combined assessments varied from 20 per cent to 80 per cent coursework. English teachers, in particular, were delighted to be able to offer 100 per cent coursework syllabuses and proudly demonstrated the high quality of their pupils' work in comparison to that produced in traditional, timed examinations. If there was ever a golden age of curriculum and assessment at 16-plus, the early years of the GCSE examination fitted this description.

Sadly, there was a right-wing backlash against coursework, and especially against English syllabuses with 100 per cent coursework. This reached its nadir in November 1991 when the Prime Minister, John Major, without any consultation with teachers, announced a limit of 20 per cent on coursework in examinations. English teachers were by then at war with the Government about key stage 3 tests, which were of very low quality in their early years. The lack of professional trust implicit in the Prime Minister's speech and in the Government's opposition to coursework in English angered many teachers. In my school, this led to the premature retirement of the head of English, one of the most gifted teachers I have ever had the privilege to meet. In a scathing letter to Lord Griffith, the chair of SEAC, he described the beneficial effects of coursework assessment in English, in contrast to the examinations which preceded it, when

> the 'O' level English literature examination became a byword for ennui. More people were deterred from reading books by that squalid examination than by television . . . Then it all changed . . . After a hundred years of virtual drought with an examination system, we enjoyed six wonderful fertile years with coursework . . . The children, able and weak, feeling that their work was more valued because they were given time and opportunity to develop it, were highly motivated and felt liberated to experiment, research and redraft. The damaging myth that it was easy to succeed in this system could not have been further from the truth . . . Real learning and real scholarship took place . . . The coursework system proved itself to be a highly efficient and sophisticated method of assessing ability in this very special subject.

Subsequently, SEAC and its successor body raised the coursework limit above 20 per cent in most subjects, but the damage done by John Major was irreparable and unforgivable.

As an examination for the whole school population, the GCSE has worked well, although there are complaints that it does not stretch the most able pupils and there remains a stubborn proportion at the lower end of the ability range who are not motivated to learn by the examination. Nevertheless, it has been a considerable improvement on GCE Ordinary level and CSE. It is a matter of regret that the Government has retreated from the principle of a single examination at 16-plus, not only through the limits placed on coursework, but also through the tiering of papers in many subjects and through the introduction of the starred A grade (i.e. higher than A grade), which has devalued the A grade and caused a large amount of unnecessary stress among the most academically able 16 year olds, who now tend to regard the A grade as a disappointment.

The pertinent question in 1999 is no longer how to develop the GCSE examination, but whether to abolish it. As the age for leaving full-time education has now effectively risen from 16 to 18, it is anachronistic to have a major school-leaving examination for 16 year olds.

TECHNICAL AND VOCATIONAL EDUCATION INITIATIVE (TVEI)

The Technical and Vocational Education Initiative (TVEI) began in 1983 as a pilot in 14 LEAs and, during the next ten years, over £1 billion was invested in TVEI schemes. At the start, TVEI was portrayed by the Government as a means to bring some sharp, efficient industrial/commercial thinking into education. It was the brainchild of Geoffrey Holland, head of the Manpower Services Commission (MSC) and later Permanent Secretary at the Departments of Employment and Education before they merged, and David Young, the MSC chair, of whom the Prime Minister, Margaret Thatcher, once famously said, 'Everyone else brings me problems; David brings me solutions'. Seen by its originators as a solution to the perceived problem of a school curriculum which did not prepare young people for the workplace, TVEI was viewed by the civil servants in the DES as an intrusion into education by another department. Teachers, after a certain amount of initial suspicion, welcomed the additional resources which came with TVEI. They were more suspicious of the growing number of non-teaching appointments as TVEI advisers, who tended to call large numbers of meetings and who rapidly acquired a new jargon and a new set of acronyms. Initially, most of the pilot schools offered TVEI courses to 14 and 15 year olds and it became a separate part of the curriculum in the upper years of secondary education, but gradually schools turned the additional resources to their advantage, purchasing computers and other expensive equipment and using TVEI not to benefit particular groups of pupils, but to underpin the whole 14–18 curriculum with TVEI principles. Indeed, TVEI was a classic example of teachers taking a central initiative, which had been planned without sufficient care or consultation, and turning it to the advantage of all their pupils.

THE NATIONAL CURRICULUM

In the first half of the 1980s, HMI and the DES had been advocating a non-statutory framework for a core curriculum, but the Prime Minister and her Secretary of State, Kenneth Baker, believed that this would give too much freedom to schools, many of which would ignore it. The Education Reform Act of 1988 therefore introduced a statutory National Curriculum. Michael Barber sees this as part of a wider programme of educational reform, which stemmed from a lack of trust in local education authorities (Barber, 1996, pp. 27–32). In the same way that grant-maintained schools, city technology colleges, local management of schools and open enrolment were intended to weaken the LEA grip on school management, the National Curriculum would reduce the influence of LEA advisers and inspectors who, with the teachers themselves, were blamed by the Government for all manner of imagined evils. At the Conservative Party Conference in the aftermath of her 1987 general election victory, Margaret Thatcher placed the blame for educational under-performance on 'hard-left education authorities and extremist teachers':

> Children who need to be able to count and multiply are learning anti-racist mathematics – whatever that may be.
>
> Children who need to be able to express themselves in clear English are being taught political slogans.
>
> Children who need to be taught to respect traditional moral values are being taught that they have an inalienable right to be gay.
>
> Children who need encouragement – and so many children do – are being taught that society offers them no future.
>
> All those children are being cheated of a sound start in life – yes, cheated.
>
> I believe that the Government must take primary responsibility for setting standards for the education of our children. That's why we are establishing a National Curriculum for basic subjects. (quoted in Barber, 1996, p. 31)

The Prime Minister wanted a National Curriculum in English, mathematics and science, but Kenneth Baker argued successfully for a broader, centrally controlled curriculum in ten subjects – English, mathematics, science, technology, history, geography, art, music, physical education and, from the age of 11, a modern foreign language – plus religious education (Graham and Tytler, 1993, p. 6).

There were many faults with the early National Curriculum and, in relation to the curriculum for 14 and 15 year olds, headteachers focused on two main criticisms. Firstly, the production of hugely detailed programmes of study for all pupils from ages 5–16 cut across the move towards a 14–19 curriculum which headteachers were already advocating (SHA, 1983; SHA, 1987). Secondly, they warned that the ten-subject National Curriculum could not be fitted into the school timetable at key stage 4 (the final two years of compulsory education). This was a simple matter of arithmetic: in a 40-period week on the school timetable, preparation for GCSE in each subject took four periods. With two GCSEs in English, two in science and GCSEs in seven other National Curriculum subjects, plus physical education, religious education and careers education, this represented about 120 per cent of the time available in a typical school week, even without popular optional subjects such as business studies or a second foreign language. At key stage 4, the National Curriculum was a quart which simply would not fit into the pint pot of the school week.

This was a message which the Government did not wish to hear and Kenneth Baker raced ahead with the Education Reform Act largely in its original form. Successive Secretaries of State repeatedly tried to solve the time conundrum at key stage 4, but Baker had left them an impossible inheritance. John MacGregor introduced short courses (half-GCSEs to be awarded on the basis of 50 per cent of normal GCSE study time) and combined courses in more than one subject. He raised the question that some National Curriculum subjects could be dropped at key stage 4 and his successor, Kenneth Clarke, made music and art optional and permitted students to take either history or geography or a course combining both. The 'nightmare' of key stage 4, as Duncan Graham, the first chief executive of the NCC, describes it, was a model for all that was wrong with the introduction of the National Curriculum – Ministers who did not listen, civil servants who did not understand (because they knew little about the organisation of secondary schools) and a hugely over-prescriptive curriculum (Graham and Tytler, 1993, pp. 83–94). Even with the changes introduced by Clarke, schools found it very difficult to plan a sensible key stage 4 curriculum and the SCAA belatedly produced a booklet of guidance on key stage 4 curriculum models (SCAA, 1995). The key stage 4 curriculum remains an uneasy compromise between the broad National Curriculum for children up to the age of 14 and the over-specialisation post-16.

POST-16 EDUCATION

As the curriculum at key stage 4 was neither sensible nor practical, it is hardly surprising that little attention had been given by the Government to the relationship between pre-16 and post-16 curriculum structures. The development of post-16 education during the period 1979–97 was dominated by two Government policies: the application of market forces to education and the preservation of the GCE Advanced level at all costs. The first of these led to the incorporation of colleges as independent institutions and the encouragement of an increasing number of small sixth forms in grant-maintained 11–16 schools. The second led to the growth of a three-track qualifications system, in which general vocational qualifications were established to fill the gap between academic and occupational accreditation systems. No transfer was possible between the three tracks and proposals for a more unified system, which had a wide measure of support, were rejected by the Government.

Prior to 1979, several attempts had been made to broaden post-16 studies through the introduction of a two-tier examination system. The Q and F proposals in 1969, the N and F proposals in 1974 and the Intermediate levels in 1979 all failed to command sufficient support, mainly on the grounds that they would erode the standard, and hence the value, of A level.

In 1987, Kenneth Baker introduced the Advanced Supplementary (AS) examination. This was to contain half the content of an A-level syllabus, but would be assessed at full A level standard. The theory behind the reform was that those doing three A levels would broaden their studies by doing an additional AS course, or by doing two full A levels and two AS courses. It was even suggested that some students might do six AS courses instead of three A levels. The take-up of AS courses made a slow start, because schools were not confident that university admission tutors would give adequate recognition to the AS as half an A level. There is a widely held view among sixth form and college tutors that the level of understanding of the qualifications system among university admission tutors is poor and that it takes several years for a new qualification to acquire the recognition which it deserves. Anecdotal evidence of this circulated widely after the introduction of the AS. A further problem with the AS was that syllabuses contained half the content of an A level, but generally required the full range of A level skills. Consequently, students doing two AS courses were attempting a much more demanding programme than those doing one A level. As its disadvantages became more apparent, the number of candidates taking AS courses, apart from general studies, dwindled to a point where it became inevitable that the AS would have to be replaced.

THE HIGGINSON REPORT

The terms of reference of the Higginson Committee referred to 'the Government's commitment to retain A level as an essential means for setting standards of excellence' (DES, 1988), but the committee nevertheless recommended that A levels should become leaner and tougher, so that students could study five subjects after the GCSE. The Prime Minister, Margaret Thatcher, is said to have been personally responsible for the decision to reject the Higginson proposals. The attempt by the Government and SEAC to promote the AS as an alternative method of broadening the post-16 curriculum was a failure. Schools and colleges were deeply disappointed by the lack of progress towards a broader 16–19 curriculum but, beyond some lukewarm encouragement of their students to take one or two AS subjects, there was little that could be done; the imperative was to ensure that students were successful in their university applications and this continued, throughout the period of the Conservative Government, to mean an increasingly high set of A-level grades. General studies and other courses, some accredited, some uncertificated, remained the means to bring breadth to the study programmes of most students.

VOCATIONAL COURSES

The most significant change to the post-16 curriculum came not through a broadening of the academic curriculum, but through the general vocational courses, widely available from the mid-1980s. Up to then, one-year post-16 courses had been offered, mainly in colleges, from the City and Guilds, the Business and Technician (later, Technology) Council (BTEC) and the Royal Society of Arts (RSA). The leader in the field was the Certificate of Pre-Vocational Education (CPVE), but, although this was a flexible general qualification, it foundered because it had no clear progression routes. The CPVE was developed by City and Guilds into the Diploma of Vocational Education (DoVE) at three levels, by which time BTEC had introduced the BTEC First Diploma in a number of broad vocational areas. Although schools were not permitted to offer the BTEC First until the early 1990s, they were quick to move into the field of one-year post-16 qualifications, seeing these as a means of attracting a broader spectrum of students into the sixth form. The incorporation of colleges and the consequent breakdown in local post-16 curriculum planning and cooperation accelerated the pace of this development.

From the viewpoint of many students, there was a yawning gap between Advanced level courses and job-related vocational qualifications. The bringing together of the CPVE and BTEC First into a three-tier system of General National Vocational Qualifications (GNVQ) filled this gap and created a marketplace for schools and colleges to fight for student enrolments. By the mid-1990s, most schools with sixth forms and all further education colleges were providing a good range of GNVQ courses at Intermediate and Advanced levels. In the public mind, however, GNVQ courses are a poor second best to Advanced levels and it is still the case that few students with the academic ability to succeed at Advanced level take GNVQ courses, although most institutions organise the curriculum in such a way that students can take one A-level and one GNVQ Advanced course.

Vocational courses have formed a smaller part of the pre-16 curriculum, although the GNVQ Part 1 courses, usually taking 20 per cent of curriculum time, are offered in many schools.

GNVQ courses have provided schools with the means to increase the size of their sixth forms, although the complex GNVQ acceditation and assessment regime has greatly increased the workload of the teachers leading the courses. It has been more difficult for schools to decide whether to offer the GNVQ Part 1 at key stage 4, since there are inherent dangers that only the least academically able students will take the courses and hence they will have lower self-esteem – exactly the reverse of what is required for these young people. Nevertheless, those schools which include GNVQ Part 1 at key stage 4 have found that the courses offer a sound and motivating experience.

THE DEARING REPORT

The problems of the overcrowded National Curriculum programmes of study at key stages 1 and 2, and the extraordinarily complex assessment system were becoming daily more apparent and, in 1993, the Secretary of State, John Patten, asked Sir Ron (now Lord) Dearing to conduct a review of the whole National Curriculum. At key stages 1 to 3, the problems were clear and Dearing did much to solve these in his report (Dearing, 1994). The evidence which he received about key stage 4 reflected the division of opinion within the profession between those who advocated a broad, balanced curriculum across all National Curriculum subject areas and those who wanted greater flexibility and subject choice for young people of this age group. His limited proposals represented an uneasy compromise between these viewpoints. At key stage 4, even more than at the earlier key stages, Dearing offered a pragmatic solution without the rationale or coherence which should underpin a national curriculum.

Meanwhile, pressure was growing for reform of the post-16 qualifications structure. In *A British Baccalaureat* (IPPR, 1990), the Institute for Public Policy Research had put forward a radical solution for a broader post-16 curriculum. The National Commisssion on Education (1993) proposed a broad scheme for the 14–19 age group. Many other bodies, including the Royal Society, the Royal Society of Arts and the Confederation of British Industry, produced papers on 16–19 education. College principals and secondary headteachers, of both maintained and independent schools produced a brief, but influential, paper *Post-Compulsory Education and Training* (Association Colleges *et al.*, 1994), and this finally persuaded the Secretary of State, Gillian Shephard, to ask Dearing to conduct a second inquiry. In *A Review of Qualifications for 16 to 19 Year Olds* (1996), Dearing's recommendations were constrained by his terms of reference, which prevented much change to A levels and preserved the academic/vocational divide that has bedevilled the English and Welsh qualifications system for generations.

The Labour Government postponed the introduction of the Dearing reforms in order to carry out a consultation on post-16 qualifications, *Qualifying for Success* (DfEE, 1997b). This was a very tentative document and, when the reforms were finally announced in 1998, they were a pale shadow of the radical measures which were required. The reformulated AS (now called Advanced Subsidiary) is a great improvement on Kenneth Baker's original AS, and there are some useful amendments to GNVQs and to the modular accreditation system, but little else to excite school and college leaders who have been campaigning vigorously for a unified framework of qualifications, based on a modular structure and embracing with equal esteem academic and vocational courses.

In Scotland, after nine years of debate and a search for a consensus solution, the *Higher Still* (SOED, 1994) reforms are on the point of introduction. In Wales, the proposals for a Welsh Baccalaureat received a cautious welcome from Welsh Office Ministers. Yet it seems that, in England, the old battles still have to be fought and the politicians of both major parties are not prepared to address the central problem of A level, beside which all other qualifications seem to be regarded as second best by opinion-formers and parents. There is still a long road to coherence and it will take much greater courage than has yet been shown by the Government if we are to travel sufficiently far down this road.

6

SCHOOLS IN DEPRIVED AREAS

PAT COLLINGS

THE CONTEXT

Sandwiched as Sinfin Community School was in 1984 between the parliamentary constituencies of Margaret Beckett and Edwina Currie, the school could hardly fail to provide its new headteacher with contrasting political and personal styles on the doorstep. Who could have foreseen the tragedies and comedies which were to change the course of their political lives over my 13 years in post? I was given an early indication of where any genuine support was to come from. Derbyshire headteachers learned to avoid attracting Mrs Currie's attention, since she tended to provide the ever-receptive local evening paper with brickbats to throw particularly at those who, like me, were managing schools serving deprived areas of the city of Derby and elsewhere. Mrs Beckett and her office, meanwhile, never failed to acknowledge and work on problems to which I alerted her or to take determined action on behalf of individual constituents; she even kept a long-standing diary engagement to visit Sinfin School, despite being catapulted by John Smith's death into being leader of Her Majesty's Opposition. Who could have predicted the major reforms of successive Conservative administrations, which were to transform large areas of the work that I was appointed to do?

Unusually for the time, Derbyshire local education authority provided incoming headteachers with a well-planned induction course. I well remember John Evans, then Director of Education for Derbyshire, assuring the group that whatever decisions the Education Committee might make, it would be our practice in schools which would have the real impact on teaching and ultimately on the children's education. Throughout the years, I hung on, sometimes grimly, to that concept of being a gatekeeper to the most significant of children's experience in formal education – the classroom process – the personal chemistry between teacher and learner.

In this chapter I shall inevitably draw on personal experience, confident that much of it was replicated in other British schools serving areas of significant social deprivation. Headteachers of such schools, both within a local area and in national gatherings, have a special affinity. They support each other of necessity, not least during the period of Conservative Government when constrained by the prevailing punitive climate to tell our true stories in private. Hence, feelings of isolation and potential or actual depression could be relieved by sharing the latest unbelievable episode in managing the effects of poverty, violence, crime, social exclusion, racism, abuse, rape or simply social ineptitude. Headteachers from schools serving more salubrious areas readily volunteered that their jobs did not resemble ours and that their skills and capabilities would be inadequate to cope with the pressures and dilemmas presented on a daily basis to management teams in schools serving stressed communities. One of our number once quipped, 'We do regular headship as well!'

As matters worsened from the early 1990s, I called a meeting of agencies working in the Sinfin community in order to identify and analyse the problems and to present a unified case for special help; it was small comfort that my analysis of a community in crisis was supported by the other agencies who all felt they were struggling to turn, or even cope with, the social tide.

It was my experience during the Conservative era, borne out by statistical evidence, that the external factors which militated against schools in deprived areas doing their best for all their pupils became more and more concentrated in a significant number of city schools. This occurred as a direct result of policies designed to put schools into the marketplace. These policies were based on the principle of providing the customers (parents) with choice in their 'purchase' of school places, with all that implies in terms of competition and cost effectiveness.

Bleak housing estates with a high percentage of temporary occupancy, endemic unemployment, lone parenting, traumatised families, high juvenile crime and involvement in the drugs and substance abuse scene are familiar characteristics of socially deprived areas. With notable exceptions, schools in such areas are represented in the lowest league-table rankings. So what are the indicators of social deprivation which may have a strong influence on pupil performance in the secondary sector? The odds are stacked against children achieving their potential when:

- prior achievement in reading (at the end of primary education) is below chronological age for more than 90 per cent of the intake;
- there is a 20 per cent change in the roll of children in year 7 alone;
- there are from 20 to 90 children with statements of special need;
- some children are the principal carers in their family;
- bilingual children are not receiving the level of support they need to reach their potential;
- child-protection procedures have been applied to 8 per cent of the school population;
- a declining school roll forces a school to be a net receiver of children excluded from other schools for anti-social behaviour;
- violent assaults by adults on staff or children become a daily fear and an all too frequent reality.

Even the most optimistic amongst us knows that, in such circumstances, the school is the inadequate glue in the social fabric of a neighbourhood. Aware of the levels of aggression surrounding such schools, local police who become frequent visitors are wont to declare that they 'wouldn't have your job'. Such environmental factors cannot but influence children's achievements.

It was not until the ghastly killing of the London headteacher Philip Lawrence outside his own school gates that the general public became aware of the dangers faced by children and staff in some schools. A significant number of headteachers thought, 'There but for the grace of God . . .' I had personally removed a gun from a holiday intruder; had been threatened and subsequently physically assaulted by a parent; had had to barricade myself in my room against another would-be attacker who was eventually removed in handcuffs; and had witnessed violent attacks by parents on their own children. Other headteachers told similarly hair-raising tales of narrow escapes. We could all accept and embrace that schools do make a difference (Mortimore *et al.*, 1988), but that poor examination results were the sole responsibility of teachers was a hard pill to swallow.

It seemed clear to me that Conservative education policies were working against each other: while wanting to drive up measurable standards, some of the very tools helping schools to support the essential learning climate were being removed.

THE CURRICULUM

The Technical and Vocational Education Initiative (TVEI) was, despite concerns about the proportion of money reaching schools, increasingly successful in its aim of sharing good practice in and between schools, setting targets and measuring outcomes. The 1983 pilot project schools were followed by a phased introduction nationwide; even highly sceptical education authorities such as Derbyshire eventually joined. The initiative helped significantly to relate the processes by which children learn to their achievements. Personal and social education, including issues relating to gender and race, were given a suitably high profile. Information technology was given a real boost: homes in deprived areas were rarely equipped with the latest hardware and children could have access to computers only in school.

Many teachers involved in local working groups with colleagues from other schools, colleges of further education and special schools were professionally enriched and stimulated by debate. Back at school, they managed change in the knowledge that accountability for appropriate use of funding would be accompanied by informed recognition of their work. Middle managers were able to enhance their promotion prospects by taking lead roles in the consortium and in the wider LEA network. At its best, TVEI enabled sensitive information to be shared between schools as well as resources, equipment and expertise. Collaboration was tempered with a healthy competitive edge. Schools in deprived areas were thus well supported by this initiative until the creation of grant-maintained (GM) schools. There was then much bad blood between schools, particularly in cities where the decision to opt out was often construed by those remaining within the LEA as a betrayal, conniving at the unfair redistribution of scarce resources and putting further obstacles in the path of struggling schools. In the case of the TVEI, opting out in turn led to the sudden or gradual withdrawal of schools from consortia, disproportionately depleting their funds, but more significantly, breaking the collaborative mould which had been the hallmark of success in this initiative.

The arrival of the General Certificate of Secondary Education (GCSE), introduced as a single subject examination system to students in 1988, was a welcome development although it put all secondary teachers under additional strain. At Sinfin, detailed preparation was managed with professional determination to introduce this reform successfully. Comprehensive schools in deprived areas welcomed and defended the integration of examination systems at 16-plus as an equitable development, seeing opportunities to raise the expectations and the recognition of the achievements of the majority of their students and to challenge the received wisdom on the value and reliability of pure end-of-course academic assessment. Teachers played their part willingly in selling this development to parents and would-be employers. The so-called 'Mode 3' examinations allowed schools, irrespective of intake, to take a leading role in syllabus compilation and moderation; Sinfin's name became inextricably linked with a creative textiles examination in this way.

The success of these major reforms was due in large measure to the involvement of teachers in practical development of the initiatives after their inception; this was an inclusive time, especially important for teachers working in stressed communities where social conditions were not improving. So it was inevitable that the imposition of the ill-conceived National Curriculum Orders (for implementation of all Curriculum subjects) should be greeted with derision and that precious professional energy should be diverted into lengthy critical responses (I recall science, English, history and geography causing near apoplexy). Some of the principles of the National Curriculum were particularly welcome in mobile populations such as ours: the benefits of continuity and progression for our students and teachers were obvious, but the way in which the reform was managed dented teachers' confidence. The recording process, for example, became ever more surreal: one staffroom in a local primary school was swathed in brightly colour-coded record sheets, the complexity of which defied belief. A truly unworkable whole-school statistical return was given short shrift in secondary schools and was swiftly withdrawn but the damage was enormous: trust between Government and schools was lost. As the expensive, glossy, hard-backed folders, so soon to be obsolete, were delivered by juggernaut, funding was being squeezed at local level and the freedom of 'capped' local authorities such as Derbyshire to distribute school budgets with special indicators for social disadvantage was eroded. The introduction and subsequent revision of the National Curriculum was a conspicuously costly exercise. New Labour must surely learn the stark lesson from this damaging affair: that, in resource terms alone, imposition is wasteful. Winning the confidence of teachers pays dividends.

There were inevitable casualties of an over-prescriptive National Curriculum coinciding with decreased funding in schools. The debate about curriculum content became urgent, not least in relation to the arts which were clearly at risk in view of their exclusion from the core curriculum. Defence of arts subjects for all children was strong in many schools serving deprived areas. Recognition of their core value in giving young people much-needed opportunities – through art, music, drama and dance – to succeed, to be creative and to experience the aesthetic in their own and other cultures, to express feelings in a secure environment, to explore issues highly relevant to their everyday lives, was sharpest in such schools. I believe that an arts education is essential in providing the very attributes Britain requires in its citizens, especially those from less favoured areas: creative thought, the ability to work in a group, adaptability, tolerance and understanding of others. A secure place for the arts in a New Labour review of the National Curriculum is surely essential.

Teachers in challenging schools were among the most vociferous in opposition to the requirement of the 1988 Education Reform Act to include an act of collective worship, 'mainly Christian' in character, on a daily basis for every pupil. The notion of worship is incompatible with enforcement, we argued. Most of us chose to define spirituality in our multifaith and atheist communities in as broad a way as the law and our consciences would allow. In schools facing the realities of difficult lives there is no place for creating dissent among faith groups. This issue is, paradoxically, so controversial that no further changes have yet been proposed by either the Conservative or the Labour Government. When a review of this obligation takes place, as it inevitably will, the Labour Government should be bold in making the interpretation of the law flexible for each school's individual circumstances.

THE TEACHERS

The control emphasis was evident in policies and practices introduced during the Conservative era which affected the education workforce, especially teachers. Teaching is generally acknowledged to be very demanding work and I always feel that there is something special about staff who choose to work with disadvantaged children since there will certainly be additional demands, not least emotionally. Teachers who had always given time well beyond the school day at Sinfin were devastated by the the new pay and conditions of service (1987), which demanded that 1,265 hours should be accounted for as working hours in a school year. This represented many fewer hours than they had been working prior to union action in the mid-1980s. It took a long time for some teachers to stop keeping a personal record of hours worked; they felt undervalued and demoralised by this public doubt about their integrity.

Low teacher morale persisted nationally. Fewer graduates entered postgraduate teacher training and this was to have a disproportionately serious effect in schools in deprived areas, especially when school performance tables were introduced giving only raw statistics. In subjects which had a national shortage when vacancies arose, it became very difficult to attract and appoint suitable candidates in the more challenging schools. This applied at various times from 1986 to modern foreign languages, technology, the sciences, even geography, English and physical education. Continuity and stability for the children who needed it most were disrupted; sometimes a series of temporary appointments had to be made and some schools were even forced to reorganise the curriculum.

Like many headteachers, I considered support for teachers in training to be a professional duty, even a professional entitlement, the benefits being mutual. At Sinfin School, we had long worked in successful partnership with schools of education in initial teacher training; indeed I had had to make the case for our school to be considered as the excellent teacher training ground it proved to be. And so we entered new extended arrangements forced on training institutions in 1993, albeit with justifiable scepticism as to whether the available funding would cover our actual costs. Professionalism won the day yet again, since teachers recognised the benefits of the stimulus to themselves and ultimately to their pupils. How far such goodwill may extend is less certain.

When regulations for teacher appraisal were finally introduced in 1991, a real opportunity to restore morale by celebrating achievement in the teaching profession was lost. The mere establishment of the national appraisal project (Graham, 1996, p. 111) had led Conservative politicians to hail this as an opportunity 'to fire the vast army of lazy lefty layabouts littering our schools'. Sadly, the tone of ministerial pronouncements remained geared to appraisal as a tool for weeding out underperforming teachers and determining pay, although neither of these was in the regulations. Schools in deprived areas need, above all, a buoyant staff bursting with high self-esteem if they are to act as role models to children, some of whom have been severely damaged in this respect by their home lives. It was hardly surprising that pupil attitudes were negatively affected by the constant erosion of teacher morale. The importance of having high expectations of all pupils had been a central finding of the seminal work *School Matters* (Mortimore *et al.*, 1988). Pupils also learn profound lessons from the ethical character of schools (National Commission on Education, 1993, p. 40). That Government should have high expectations of teachers in a supportive climate was clearly not understood by successive Conservative Secretaries of State.

The issue of access to the agreed curriculum for bilingual children was a constant concern for schools serving communities with a significant proportion of children from ethnic minorities, often housed in the less desirable areas of a city. The funding mechanism was via Section 11 Home Office project grants distributed according to tight criteria related to linguistic competence, i.e. for work with children whose first language was not English. Community expectations were very high but there was a dearth of appropriately qualified applicants and contracts were temporary; some dedicated staff achieved excellent results, but were distressed as the annual budget cuts resulted in deletion of posts and late renewal of contracts. This funding anomaly was at best inefficient and, with less secure conditions of service, created problems in a highly sensitive area. New Labour should bring such funding into the mainstream – there are adequate mechanisms to ensure accountability through existing channels.

STANDARDS AND QUALITY

It is widely acknowledged that good leaders keep a delicate balance between pressure and support in order to draw the best out of their workforce. As an innovating school we had received a fair degree of attention from HMI in the form of individual visits to look at, for example, our induction programme for new staff, a language awareness course, and a teacher training partnership in humanities. Like many of my colleagues, I welcomed the professional exchanges which accompanied these visits, but found my respect edged with anxiety when we were one of the few schools in the autumn of 1989 to receive a few weeks' notice of a so-called 'short inspection' to examine the work of some departments in depth. In the event, the quality and usefulness of the reporting outweighed the stress. We were therefore in a better position than most to compare the experience with a full school inspection by an Ofsted team in the spring of 1994. The preparatory work, especially the bureaucracy, dominated the whole term, distracting us from our central purpose rather than focusing our energies on the school. The experience and quality of individual inspectors were varied and some revealed strange misconceptions. There was an expression of surprise that our school site looked so attractive given the social information supplied about the school, but a genuine, thankfully small, fire at the start of the inspection week brought us acclaim for an orderly evacuation! The Ofsted report format at the time began each section with standards achieved in relation to national norms; for schools in socially deprived areas, this was depressing and indicative of the general mood of despondency. So many negative messages about our work influenced a disproportionate number of good teachers in stressed neighbourhoods to seek early retirement.

Not least of the morale-sapping policies was the publication of performance tables from 1992. For apparently lower-achieving schools, which had valid statistical evidence of the progress of their students since entry, it was particularly galling to be castigated by national newspapers, as well as by the local press. More importantly, some parents in socially deprived areas found it difficult to interpret the information, causing misunderstandings that, for example, grades A to C were all that an individual pupil could attain.

SCHOOLS IN THE MARKETPLACE

Even before league tables, the prevailing climate reinforced the notion of absolute standards: in its first edition *The Good Schools Guide* included Sinfin and other schools in deprived areas. We were pleased and proud, until the local press heralded this achievement on the front page with two contrasting juxtaposed photographs. One picture was of children looking rather untidy and whooping for joy (as, no doubt, instructed by the photographer) and the other, posed perhaps, of blazered, briefcase-carrying youngsters from a school in the leafy suburbs which had not been included in the *Guide*. The caption was 'Which school would you rather send your child to?' This was a damaging event, but indicates admirably the climate induced by Conservative attitudes. The Labour Government's early 'naming and shaming' of so-called 'failing' schools shocked many of us who had waited in the hope of a more supportive climate.

Like many schools, we had striven to make year-on-year improvement to our information for future pupils and parents but, with the introduction of parental preference in the Education Reform Act of 1988, we were catapulted unwillingly into a world where the cost of marketing had to be set against the income generated by each individual child. Decisions as to whether to compete with the glossy brochure style of schools that had so recently been our partners, but were now competitors, became crucial to the survival of the school. This was particularly difficult in cities which had surplus places due to demographic trends and especially where grant-maintained schools, or even a spanking new, generously resourced city technology college, were in direct competition. Local education authorities could no longer reorganise schools without facing the inevitable consequences: a move to opt out of local authority control in favour of grant-maintained status by any school threatened with closure.

How to 'market' the particular successes of a school in a disadvantaged area, in a climate where league-table position was the overriding public perception of success, was really testing. After highlighting areas of examination success, should we be honest and proclaim our wealth of experience and success in providing for children with learning difficulties, or our relative success in dealing with severely disturbed or disruptive pupils or those whose stay was of limited duration? If so, we would certainly not attract more of the very parents of children whose presence was needed for the balanced intake within which we could provide the best for all children. Special skills developed by teachers would not extend to a majority with particular difficulties. Or should we omit any references to these real areas of strength? How much time should we devote to taking the school's display stands or slide show or video out into the primary schools? Wasn't our first duty to our existing pupil population? Schools in disadvantaged areas did not seem able to stem the tide of aspirant families seeking places in more middle-class settings. The notion of success, defined as adding value or progressing beyond expectation, did not win the battle for applicants.

Schools in deprived areas were dealt a double blow by the new definition of parental choice and the subsequent free-for-all. One of the benefits of the National Curriculum had been to sharpen existing cross-phase curriculum liaison groups between secondary schools and their partner primary schools to the benefit of children and staff. Now, not only did all offers of support and cross-phase work have to be vetted with an eye on public relations, but primary schools no longer felt able to devote so much time to one secondary school as the destinations of their pupils became less and less predictable. Worse, forecasting pupil numbers for the next academic year became a nightmare. While headteachers in over-subscribed schools in the leafier suburbs had to contend with parental appeals for the places available, schools with vacant places receiving children who had not made the school their first choice had an uphill struggle to engage parents positively. Tutor groupings and induction programmes for incoming pupils were much more difficult to plan as decisions were still being made well into the summer holidays.

In neighbourhoods which displayed little confidence in themselves as communities – residents with aspirations for their families tended not to stay long nor even to acknowledge their true address – the natural response to the notion of choice was to look outside the immediate area. The grass was surely greener on the other side. Paradoxically, parents being shown around the school on a normal school day who had no previous members of the family as pupils generally pronounced favourably on the working environment. Many schools in deprived areas are indeed a haven of calm compared with the world outside the school gate. The lack of experience of state education among Conservative Ministers was nowhere more apparent than in its confused view of social deprivation as social disorder in schools.

For schools in deprived areas, the greatest effect of the marketplace was undoubtedly the loss of funds. Fewer children, generating smaller annual budgets, disguised the fact that pupil turnover in such schools was often high; families in traumatic situations were frequently unstable and transient residents. Budget formulae were not sufficiently flexible to accommodate this syndrome and some schools suffered disproportionately. The situation was exacerbated by an overall diminution of funds from 1992, putting ever more pressure on LEAs to delete or downgrade social deprivation supplements from their funding formulae. Such positive discrimination was not a feature of Conservative policy nationally. Many headteachers campaigned forcefully for differential funding while recognising the increasingly depressing financial picture for all schools.

At the chalkface, the result of the financial cuts was an annual round of preparation for redundancies; a massive investment of management and governor time; early retirement of nearly all staff over 50 years old; the deletion of posts across the curriculum including vital learning support posts; no more free music instrument tuition; real cuts in departmental allowances; refurbishment reduced to a minimum; and many more examples. By 1990, the possibility of being creative with community funding had long since gone and there was no place in an LMS budget for overlapping activity. This was extremely short-sighted, as the climate for learning in a community such as ours with fewer than average successful adult role models needed to demonstrate as much formal learning by adults. The indirect benefits of adults learning alongside children were incalculable.

THE PUPILS

First impressions of a school in a deprived area often lead to discussions about the relative size of pupils, their diets and general physical development. In my time as a headteacher, insufficient attention was paid to these real and sometimes urgent issues. In a so-called 'affluent society' it was difficult to equate the trappings of high-spending yuppies with the hunger of poor children. Teachers in poor areas were used to supplying food and gifts of clothing for some children to enable them to digest food for the mind.

It was abundantly clear to me that early pre-school support was needed in communities like Sinfin in order to counter the effects of disadvantage. Primary school colleagues were having to help children acquire basic social and linguistic skills on arrival in reception classes. Some LEAs tried to maintain the commitment to nursery education, but the Conservative administration did not embrace this as a policy to counter underachievement, despite research findings on the efficacy of enrichment programmes.

Of course, many children succeeded against the odds with the support of excellent teaching and so it was galling for those who progressed to post-16 education elsewhere in the city to be taunted about coming from an area which was notorious for its crime rates and other less celebratory social statistics. The league tables were failing in their aim to drive up standards in the very areas where it mattered most and they did such students no favours – the struggle to succeed became even more difficult.

A handful of parents in the Sinfin area entered their academically bright children for independent school places. Comments from receiving schools were highly complimentary on their education over three years at Sinfin. At the other end of the scale, the placement of children with special needs according to parental choice resulted in a number of children entering mainstream schools against professional advice. Again, it was up to willing but ever more burdened teachers to meet the very special needs of these children; there were some spectacular successes. However, the amount of paperwork required by the SEN (Special Educational Needs) Code of Practice was excessive and especially so where numbers of children qualifying for such attention represented a high proportion of the intake. For schools in deprived areas the additional factor was the support needed for parents going through the process; they were not infrequently resistant to any help for their child, seeing it as a stigma.

Although welcome in principle, the Children Act 1991 and reformed child protection procedures in the wake of a number of shocking national cases also brought additional burdens to schools serving stressed neighbourhoods. Clear but lengthy procedures had to be followed – yet another demand on time and emotional energy with no public recognition or extra funding.

Children from ethnic minorities, meanwhile, well represented among the hard-working, well-motivated, high-achieving students, had to struggle with the straddling of two cultures, the search for a cultural identity and the maintenance of competence in two languages. Given some Conservative social policies, such as on immigration, it was not surprising that some of our pastoral work became involved with family trauma over residency in the UK or with children left as orphans without an extended family. Racism in the wider community impinged on the school in various forms, not least a vile overnight posting from outside the community of Ku Klux Klan propaganda. A great deal of work needed to be done to heal divisions in society by the end of the Conservative era.

PARENTS AND GOVERNORS

The Conservative commitment to extend the involvement of parents in their children's education brought an increase in the number of parents on governing bodies. This was welcome in principle, but in practice it was very difficult to fill the places allocated in areas such as Sinfin. While attendance at annual parent–teacher consultations was good, a lack of confidence and other pressing demands meant that few put themselves forward to serve as governors without support and encouragement from headteachers; parent governor elections were a regular occurrence and there was much work to be done behind the scenes to try to obtain a balanced representation of gender and ethnicity. Later Conservative ideas for parental involvement in the form of parent–school contracts were not well developed and generated antagonism because of the punitive overtones, appearing to hold parents to account for their offspring's behaviour.

CONCLUSION

Despite commitment to urban renewal in terms of employment and the environment, Conservative Governments have tended to see urban schools as part of the problem rather than the key to a solution (Mortimore *et al.*, 1993, p. 21). There is now a wealth of research findings on what facilitates learning, including children's views of what helps or hinders (Ruddock *et al.*, 1996) and practical analyses of what makes a school effective (MacGilchrist *et al.*, 1997). Thus the Labour Government of 1997, having education as a declared priority, needs to demonstrate a shift in the national culture. Labour's attempt to focus on learning as the central purpose of education contrasts with the previous period of constant changes in structure and governance, which left classroom practices largely unchanged. Such an agenda represents the best hope of improving the achievements of the young people in schools in deprived areas.

7

COMMUNITY SCHOOLS

ROGER SECKINGTON

Over the past 30 years, a wide variety of models for 'community schooling' have been developed within comprehensive education, the term having even more meanings than the word 'comprehensive' itself. Back in the 1960s, when comprehensive reorganisation was in its infancy, the use of the word 'community' to describe a comprehensive school was almost axiomatic, but often meant little more than making the school premises available occasionally to others, or organising older pupils for various types of community activity in the area. Over the years, and particularly since the 1970s, community practices and experiments have grown, and with them an increasingly sophisticated philosophy of community and its relationship to the twin concepts of social and educational change. One strand developed from the thinking behind the network of village colleges established by Henry Morris in Cambridgeshire; and it is this strand which is the principal focus of this chapter.

LEICESTERSHIRE COMMUNITY COLLEGES

Those of us fortunate enough to have worked in one of the five Leicestershire Phase III community colleges for the decade following their introduction in 1976 probably saw the apogee of that type of LEA-inspired community schooling. Hind Leys in Shepshed opened in 1976, followed by Earl Shilton and Groby in 1977. Babington and Moat in the city of Leicester opened in the early 1980s. These five newly designated community colleges were the pioneers in a phase of development intended to spread in time across the whole county and it is reasonable to speculate that if circumstances had not changed so dramatically there would have been further phases as the concept of fully integrated community schooling was developed.

Leicestershire's contribution to community education is generally well known but it is necessary to rehearse some of the key points in order to better understand Phase III in the context of a progressive development of community provision based on schools. Stewart Mason was only the second Director of Education for Leicestershire, following Sir William Brockington, who had served from 1902 to 1947. In 1937 Stewart Mason went to Cambridgeshire as a junior inspector of HMI; 'there he met the man who was to be one of the most important influences on his life and career, Henry Morris' (Jones, 1988, p. 26). Morris had established a number of village colleges in Cambridgeshire before the Second World War and these were used as the model by Stewart Mason in his memorandum on community education in 1949. His scheme

> envisaged three main grades of institution serving community purposes: the college of further education, carrying out the greater part of the part-time 'County College' type of education for 16–18 year olds; the 'Village College' on the Cambridgeshire pattern attached to a secondary school; and the 'Village Centre' (in towns, the Neighbourhood Centre) attached to a primary school. (Jones, 1988, p. 48)

The first community college opened in 1954 at Ivanhoe (Ashby-de-la-Zouch), at that time a secondary modern school but soon to become a high school, and very appropriately it was opened by Henry Morris.

Ashby was a Phase I community college. The head became a 'head and warden' to recognise the wider role (warden being the term used in Cambridgeshire) and a community tutor was appointed to develop adult education provision and wider use of the premises by the local community. Community tutor appointments were jointly for school and the community – notionally dividing their time 60:40 between the two. Initially, separate core facilities were added for adults (an adult wing including an adult lounge, coffee bar, committee room and office) and this enabled some daytime use and gave an appropriate social focus at times when the whole range of facilities was available for community use. From the start, both in Cambridgeshire and Leicestershire, an important principle was to make school buildings readily available for educational, recreational and cultural use by all members of the community. Often schools possess the best facilities in their local community and these were made available in the evenings, at weekends and in the holidays. Greater use of 'school' premises during the day was to come later.

By 1970 the number of Leicestershire community colleges had grown steadily into double figures. Developments were taking place all the time so each phase was not discrete. In the late 1960s and early 1970s the pace of development and addition of new colleges increased markedly. The key LEA figure in these developments was Andrew Fairbairn, first as deputy to Stewart Mason, then, from 1971, as the Director of Education. New 14–19 upper schools and community colleges were opened at Bosworth, Countesthorpe and Wreake. The design of these buildings reflected Mason's focus on curricular integration and resource-based learning. Colleges attempted to become more user-friendly for all members of the community.

Phase II was developed at this time. Crucial to staffing in Phase II colleges was the first full-time community post, a head of community education, supported by two community tutors (youth and adult), part-time teachers and youth workers and some administrative staff. These teams were responsible for substantial programmes of work with people of all ages and attempted to meet a wide range of needs.

It is important to reflect on the general support structures available to Leicestershire community workers in the early 1970s. As already mentioned, Andrew Fairbairn's leadership, enthusiasm and support for a developing programme of community work based on schools were crucial. His leadership gave a focus to community education that placed the LEA in the forefront of such initiatives. At a local level, a team of area further education officers ensured that practical support and advice were available for adult education programmes and youth work. Advisers were concerned about the quality of adult education classes and were involved in training. A network of support existed between colleges so that there was plenty of dialogue, sharing of good practice and exchange of ideas. Annual conferences ensured that some sense of the total LEA commitment to community education could be assessed as well as giving some high level in-service training opportunities. Those joining the LEA at that time would be in no doubt of the importance given to community education and that it underpinned the whole education service. That was a time when the office and the colleges worked particularly closely.

The development of the five Phase III colleges reflected their catchment, staffing and premises. For example, Moat is located on the outskirts of the city centre and has a strong multicultural dimension. The colleges were all in new buildings whose design and construction reflected the integrated approach expected of them. They were all fairly small schools, compared with some of the giant upper schools of the time, especially the three upper schools within the former Leicestershire county area, Earl Shilton, Groby and Hind Leys. However, there were several common elements which distinguished this phase as being significantly different from its predecessors. At that time, throughout the county the rather clumsy title of 'head and warden' was replaced by that of 'principal'. This is not a matter of pomp or status but a reflection of the desire to signify a unitary approach. The original title had drawn attention to a duality of organisation. Many argued then, and still do so now, that it is better to organise schools and community provision separately. However, the title 'principal' was universally adopted in Leicestershire and was a clear statement of intent to work towards a unitary service. I would identify three key features particular to the new Phase III colleges.

Vice-principals

Hitherto, the senior community appointment had been at head of department or assistant principal level and paid on further education pay scales. Now, an additional vice-principal appointment was possible. Clearly several options existed as to how the team of three or four vice principals could be organised. The best demonstration of a wholly integrated approach would have been to share the jobs and responsibilities across the team. In practice, the new colleges were anxious to recruit people with good experience of community work so as (to lift a phrase much used by the new government in 1997) to 'hit-the-streets-running'. There was great benefit in having a senior team of equals planning, co-ordinating and promoting work across the whole enterprise. The traditional divisions of responsibility such as curriculum, pastoral/ personnel, support and community tended to remain. For the many users and co-workers it was certainly easier if they knew whom to seek on a particular issue. It could be argued that an opportunity was lost to develop a vice-principal team that shared jobs and, over time, changed roles. But there is an understandable tendency in most organisations to develop a structure because it gives clarity and focuses skills and strengths where they are needed. However, vice-principals who came from a community education background joined their 'school' colleagues on equal terms and could influence whole institution planning. They thus experienced a wider base from which to develop their careers.

Budget

Following the introduction of local management of schools (LMS) and the quite aggressive environment of bidding for funding from a variety of sources, the block-finance scheme introduced in 1977 seems quite tame. At the time it was a considerable departure from the traditional LEA procedures. Each college was allocated a budget along the same lines as further education colleges. In many ways it foreshadowed the LMS of a decade later. Virement was possible between headings and the whole system allowed for good housekeeping. There was considerable advantage in direct management of repair and maintenance, the ability to make minor improvements, and to move finance from one heading to another if 'savings' had been made in one area of work that could usefully be allocated to support another part of the programme. County treasurers were perhaps understandably wary at the new freedom given to these Phase III colleges by the block finance scheme. There is no doubt that it worked well, encouraging responsible financial planning whilst giving a useful measure of local flexibility. Mutual confidence in the scheme was quickly established. The LEA remained responsible for strategic and macro-financial planning. The spectre of how to cope with flat roofs or transport in rural areas would loom later.

Community teachers

The almost explosive potential of this initiative has never been fully appreciated. If it had been allowed a period of steady development and had been adopted in an increasing number of community schools, it might have changed fundamentally the way in which community schools were organised. Regrettably, it was more expensive and at a time of increasing budgetary restraint its future was in doubt from the start.

'This new initiative meant that each member of the teaching staff had an option to take up an annually renewable community contract to work on some area of the community education programme' (Hussain and Hughes, 1995, p. 52). The notional division between the school and community contracts was 90:10. Thus, a school with 50 teachers on 90:10 community contracts would have an actual staffing of 55. 'Teaching staff with community contracts (5–10 per cent) had time off in lieu and an additional payment of £500 per annum for each 10 per cent contract' (Hussain and Hughes, 1995, p. 53). The benefit to the statutory curriculum provision, especially in the smaller community school, is obvious. At the same time, a way had been found to weave the skills, specialisms and interests within the teaching force into the fabric of the wider community programme. It would be arrogant to assume that school buildings and the teachers working in them were either the only or most important resource in the community. Most communities have a network of community assets through voluntary organisations, the church, sports clubs and the like, but schools still represent a major physical and human resource too often limited to the exclusive daytime and weekday use of a particular age group between 5 and 18.

Some community teachers were appointed as 'across-the-board' heads of department (HOD), a clumsy but fairly graphic title. Fortunately this type of appointment was also extended to a small number of Phase II colleges. Ideally, every department would be led by a head of department or head of faculty (HOF) to ensure integrated curriculum provision. In practice, two areas of work – physical and recreational activity and design – were particularly comfortable and successful with this approach. In these or any other curriculum area the HOD/HOF would be responsible for that area of work across the whole college programme, helping to appoint full-time and part-time staff, ensuring full and proper use of facilities, coordinating the whole range of activities and most importantly advising the community vice-principal on the appropriateness and quality of the programme. This was a formidable role, but one which, in my experience, was welcomed. These appointments were usually made on an 80:20 basis so that in theory there was time off in lieu for two of the daytime sessions to make up for the heavier evening, weekend and 'holiday' commitments as well as the additional community teacher payments. This arrangement worked particularly well in curriculum areas like design and physical/recreational because of the pressure by the wider community for access to the facilities and to the specialists working in these disciplines. Demand for use of swimming pools, outdoor playing areas, floodlit all-weather areas, sports halls and gymnasia by individuals or groups, either within a class programme or in direct use of facilities, nearly always outstrips availability. Apart from expressive arts, languages and commercial subjects, other subjects were not under the same pressure to respond to wider community needs, so across-the-board HOD appointments were not usually made.

Considerable flexibility existed within the community teacher scheme and each of the five colleges was able to develop its own approach. The notional 90:10 contract gave, in effect, a community teacher establishment. Since not all teachers undertook a specific community contract, some of their colleagues could have an increased proportion of their time in a community role. Some 70:30 appointments were made to give support in areas like youth work. Contracts were renewed annually and could also be used for development work. In some cases the time off in lieu may have been spread across the year, but the community element concentrated in a particular period such as summer play schemes. This was quite a challenge to a profession used to working a regular annual contract based on a well-defined working day and a carefully constructed timetable. The community teacher scheme was devised to give increased flexibility to the dual system of a team of teachers working a school day and others being employed outside those hours for adult and youth work. It was a major step towards a more holistic approach.

THE IMPACT OF CENTRALISED REFORMS

The community teacher contract was an opt-in scheme. It is interesting to speculate what might have been if the three original Phase III colleges – Hind Leys (1976), Earl Shilton (1977) and Groby (1977) – had opened in a climate that allowed for a completely fresh and highly focused start. Certainly they were all in excellent new buildings located in well-defined communities which had not previously had local post-14 secondary schools, Leicestershire having a two-tier secondary provision of 11–14 high schools and 14–19 upper schools in the pre-1974 county area. Their planning had been the result of a newly introduced process involving appropriate LEA officers, architects and some heads from neighbouring schools. The result was three well-designed, attractive and practical buildings able to give a good focus to community work. Yet there was already some caution and a hint of the difficulties for the full development of the scheme throughout the LEA that lay ahead. Some signs were already there of the gathering assault on the education service that was such a feature of the Thatcher years and beyond.

Many consider Prime Minister James Callaghan's Ruskin College speech in 1976 as opening the national debate which was to reach such vicious momentum a decade later. As a result of the Maud Report, some local government areas were reorganised in 1974. The former county of Leicestershire was enlarged to incorporate the city of Leicester and the permanently reluctant, small but historic Rutland. Rutland had already adopted a Cambridgeshire style of community provision well suited to a rural area. The city of Leicester, however, presented a quite different set of challenges with its own secondary school system, a significant multicultural dimension and the usual assets and problems of a large urban area. Working concurrently with this reorganisation I cannot claim to have been much affected by it. But even at that time it did not seem to be a change for the better and with hindsight it may be seen to have set in train some unfortunate consequences.

For many in the service at that time the enlarged LEA was one of energy, urgency almost, as an incredible range of issues was tackled with confident zeal. Inevitably, there were some costs, one of the most significant of which was the gradual weakening of the formerly strong, mutually supportive, links between the central office and the schools. In the 1960s the central LEA team could more or less be accommodated in a good-sized family house. A decade later what seemed like a small army was housed in a flagship County Hall on the outskirts of Leicester. Andrew Fairbairn's quite remarkable leadership was, very fortunately, still in place until 1984 enabling the style and commitment to remain, but it was against a background of increasing politicisation of the service, a growing bureaucracy with endless meetings and a vast outpouring of paper. Excellent, key people were too often hopelessly stretched by colleagues whose personal sense of importance in the overall scheme of things was frequently misplaced. When one of those overstretched officers (a friend in the office), still trying to deliver traditional values, was challenged with this view, he pointed out that much the same was happening in schools and colleges. True, restructuring of schools was frequent. To what extent this led to the backlash on local government a decade later historians will tell, but a weakening of the formerly strong partnership between the office and schools and colleges was gradually taking place. Despite this perhaps inevitable change in style, the LEA was still firmly in control of strategic planning and supporting a healthy community education programme.

The Houghton award of this time may not have helped in this relationship. The increase in teachers' salaries certainly dismayed some middle-tier officers and it was increasingly at this level that the first contact between school or college and the LEA office was made. More specifically to the Phase III colleges in the negotiation leading up to the establishment of the community teacher scheme, the teachers' unions were fully consulted. The potential for exploitation of teachers in a scheme trying to establish greater flexibility of the working pattern is too obvious to rehearse here. Understandably, union negotiators were anxious to ensure that it was an opt-in scheme and they also obtained an additional payment for sessions worked outside the normal school day. This payment may be judged as a skilful piece of negotiation and it was certainly welcomed by individuals opting-in. Although it eased the introduction of the scheme, it was one of the factors that led to its eventual demise. This could be sensed at the time. The original intention had been to adopt a flexible approach to the working week in which community teachers would have contracted for ten out of the 15 to 20 sessions available in a week. Had the practice been established, taken root and spread beyond the original pilot colleges, it could have been the most radical challenge in education in modern times.

The education service has been in a continuous process of budgetary restraint and the consequence has been ever-mounting pain. To refer to the cuts in community education in 1979 (something like one-third of the community budget overnight) may seem overly historic, but it significantly weakened the development of Phase III only two years into the scheme. The scheme was accepted by the majority of other community education providers at that time because it was their expectation that Phase III would eventually spread across the whole LEA. Indeed, two more colleges were still to be designated Phase III. Behind the scenes, however, doubts about the ability to have a universal Phase III programme already existed. In 1979 rumours spread through the county that the closure of community education in up to 11 community colleges was being considered as a way of achieving the required cuts. This led to a storm of protest uniting community workers and, more importantly, the users. During a single week, a lively community college would have had several thousand people using the facilities; having gained access to the learning and recreational opportunities they were not about to let go. Suddenly a surprisingly large, very articulate, part of the electorate was saying 'hands off our colleges'. The long-term importance of this in securing the future of neighbourhood community schools cannot be underestimated.

Did the Phase III community teacher scheme work? Regrettably it was more a case of what might have been rather than what was. Undoubtedly, all five colleges worked well, providing vigorous community education programmes which in some cases were of a real pioneering quality. In terms of the programme provided, many Phase II colleges were just as vigorous and often more extensive. Where there were measurable differences was in the organisation and management of Phase III, which moved college organisation further along the continuum from dual use to the goal of a fully integrated, unitary approach. Financial and premises management were unified. Everybody working in the community college had to commit themselves to a full acceptance of a wide community brief and most had a contractual involvement in part of the community programme additional to the 'school' teaching element. Furthermore, some progress was made in the challenging area of a more holistic approach to the curriculum. What the progressive development of this type of community schooling might have achieved by challenging the very basic structure of educational provision can only be a matter of speculation. A point was almost reached when it would have been possible to organise the 'school' day on a three- or even four-session basis with students selecting sessions. There were (and are) a host of difficulties such as transport, contracts of employment and servicing, but the attraction of having specialist facilities and personnel available over a longer timeframe is obvious.

COMMUNITY SCHOOLS IN THE 1990S

'Leicestershire's experiment with comprehensive community education Phase III could not be funded under LMS and it has been phased out over the last four years. Adult classes (Schedule II) are funded by the Further Education Funding Council' (Hussain and Hughes, 1995, p. 54). Community teacher contracts ceased at the end of the academic year 1994/95. It is disappointing to see that the efforts to draw school provision and community education closer together into a more unified service has suffered, with a return to a more overt duality. There was even some questioning as to whether it was worth spending extra money on the Phase III development. That denies the hope and possibilities of the late 1970s and comes only with the wisdom of hindsight as events unfolded in the 1980s and 1990s. What is so very heartening is the healthy state of community schooling in Leicestershire. The LEA is still funding core staff and is providing a framework through commissioning agreements. Community workers are using the new funding and support structures available to them. 'Despite cuts and changes, we are committed to continue to function as a college that serves the whole community. It makes what we do more relevant and therefore more effective' (Hussain and Hughes, 1995, p. 54).

Perhaps rather surprisingly, there is room for some optimism about individual schools wishing to develop as community schools. They will be on their own without the support provided by LEAs like Leicestershire at their zenith, but funding is available under a number of headings. It is necessary to make bids and this means more work for already overstretched school and college managers. Some even argue that aspiring schools may benefit by coming fresh to the process without the clutter of already established schemes. Certainly any development of this kind will be bottom-up and will arise from a considered local scheme placing ownership with the school and community. An invaluable resource for schools seeking to develop in this way is *Managing Schools in the Community* by Phil Street (1997).

The Education Act of 1944 laid down that

> it shall be the duty of the local education authority for every area, so far as their powers extend, to contribute towards the spiritual, moral, mental and physical development of the community by securing that efficient education throughout those stages shall be available to meet the needs of the population of their area. (Education Act 1944, Section 7, p. 4)

This was hardly a powerful mandate for community schooling but nonetheless, it set a clear framework from which a process of lifelong learning could be incorporated into the existing school system. 'The Act in fact sought to promote many of the activities which Henry Morris had been practising for many years in his village colleges' (Jones, 1988, p. 47). There was no widespread national response to this opportunity, but Stewart Mason, in his 1949 memorandum on community education, built on this statutory provision and started the process that was to lead to the eventual establishment of Leicestershire's community schooling programme.

Since 1944, despite all the plethora of legislation, there has been no significant reference to community schooling and no enabling legislation leading to a universal and vigorous system of community schools. There has been both an absence of national direction in establishing community schooling and, indirectly, the emasculation of LEAs from the mid-1980s onwards with the imposition of greater central control and the introduction of LMS, which has made regional community education schemes difficult if not impossible to implement. With all their faults, LEAs are more in touch with their communities and are often able to meet perceived needs imaginatively and creatively. The School Standards and Framework Act 1998 introduces three categories of state school: community, aided and foundation. This misinterprets the word 'community' and, tragically, diminishes the description implied by a genuine comprehensive neighbourhood community school.

The Labour Government has strongly supported the concept of lifelong learning, but has so far been reluctant to face up to the consequences of this in resource terms. Following the Kennedy Report (1998), a White Paper was promised, but failed to appear. Francis Wheen wrote:

> The White Paper was due to be published yesterday. But last week while it was at the printers, the plug was pulled: Ministers had belatedly realised than an expansion of 'lifelong education' might entail 'cash

> commitments'. Well of course it would. A report last June by the New Labour peer Helena Kennedy QC included a whole chapter headed 'Funding is the most important lever for change'. A document from David Blunkett's own National Advisory Group for Continuing Education, published in November, concluded that over the lifetime of this Parliament, the aim should be step by step to increase the total volume of funding deployed to support lifelong learning. (*Guardian*, 11 February 1998)

No mention of community schools having a role in this! Practice failing to match rhetoric has been all too common in post-war educational provision and only some LEAs and individual institutions have achieved real success with forms of community schooling which support lifelong learning.

Very recently, as a governor of the lively, local comprehensive school, I was invited to meet our newly elected MP. Clearly, he is a very intelligent man, a good listener, obviously hardworking, probably a rising star in his party and considered a good constituency MP, yet the mantra of cost-effectiveness and an apparent unreadiness to consider meeting local needs (for example, over transport difficulties in remote rural communities) except by the application of national formula, soon emerged. Oh for a Henry Morris who established a workable system of community schooling in Cambridgeshire, or a Stewart Mason who developed these ideas in Leicestershire or an Andrew Fairbairn who established Phase III in the optimistic 1970s, only to see their work fall victim to the pressures of centralised reforms in the 1980s and 1990s. They were splendid examples of educational leaders with vision, the ability to enthuse and who, through the LEA framework, achieved so much to promote lifelong education through community schooling. 'Perhaps what we really lack is any sense of education as a whole-life activity or a whole community responsibility; and as so often come back to the true community school as the answer' (Sallis, 1998, p. 66).

8

A VIEW FROM LONDON

TAMSYN IMISON

In 1979, I was thrilled to be appointed to the post of head of year 3 (i.e. 13–14 year olds, now called year 9) at Pimlico School under the inspired leadership of Kathleen Mitchell. I was also excited to be joining the Inner London Education Authority (ILEA). This was the Authority that HMI in 1980 described as 'a caring and generous Authority with considerable analytical powers to identify problems, the scale of which is, in some cases, unique in this country. It frequently pilots imaginative or innovative approaches' (DES, 1980b).

This was an Authority which commissioned David Hargreaves to write a report on good practice (Hargreaves, 1984) and then appointed him as chief inspector. It was the authority who had all the giants and the gurus such as Bill Stubbs, Peter Newsam, Sir Ashley Bramhall, Anne Sofer, Mair Garside, Tim Brighouse and Tessa Blackstone. It was the authority whose senior inspector, Denis Felsenstein, pioneered support for women managers. It was the authority with a unique research and statistics unit under Desmond Nuttall and Peter Mortimore. It was an authority that took seriously gender and race issues (ILEA, 1983), and had had to manage huge falls in pupil rolls. It was the place where all exciting teachers wanted to teach. I was not disappointed. I have never worked harder than as a teacher in Inner London but I have also never had so many rewarding outcomes and so much professional support and development.

However, in his address to the people of London in his bid to be the new mayor, Lord Archer stated: 'London's education provision is poor. They have the lowest school exam results' (Archer, 1998, p. 9). Have I been here before? As a senior manager in London schools since 1979 I have been aware of an unrelenting pressure to cut money from education and to denigrate teachers and local authorities, especially in London. Archer does go on in a footnote to admit that 'when considering the allocation of extra funds to London's schools, one must consider the much higher proportion of E2L [English as a second language] pupils in London than in the rest of the country and, secondly, the higher proportion of special needs pupils in London' (Archer, 1998).

As headteacher for 14 years at Hampstead School (really Cricklewood High!), a large London inner-city mixed comprehensive school, which matches Lord Archer's footnote, I have been setting targets and monitoring indicators such as staying-on rates and examination results related to intake levels. These have all shown a steady improvement. In 1984, Hampstead School was a violent, aggressive, ugly and unwelcoming place which allowed children to opt out of vital areas of skill, knowledge and understanding at 14 and valued only a small minority of the children. In 1998, it is a school where all students are represented, valued, known, achieve well in examinations and want to go on learning after the age of 16. All receive a broad and balanced range of knowledge and skills to support them in whatever career they choose.

During this period there have been significant changes in the Hampstead School intake, with many more students having little or no English – a change from 17 per cent in 1983 to 29 per cent in 1987 and 58 per cent in 1998. The school also has many more students with significant special needs, including two with Down's Syndrome; each class has at least three children with statements of special educational need.

Like all London schools, we have managed these changes against the following backdrop of significant external factors:

- government attacks on the ILEA, including the capping of expenditure, which resulted in a significant reduction in financial provision;
- nationally sanctioned industrial action by teachers, 1984–86, cutting off consultation between teachers, management, students and parents and regularly closing schools and impacting on children's learning;
- London National Union of Teachers unofficial action, 1986–89, which was never controlled either by the national union or by the ILEA;
- the London Identification of Teacher Exercise, where teachers above authorised numbers were formally identified as surplus to staffing requirements and were left without a permanent timetable or moved from one school to another;
- abolition of the ILEA and the move into small unitary authorities,

despite a ballot of parents showing 90 per cent in favour of retention;
- local authority reluctance to support headteachers who were trying to eradicate incompetency and unacceptable conduct against strong and effective union defence;
- changes to the pay and conditions of service requiring teachers to follow the reasonable requirements of the head;
- introduction of local management of schools;
- introduction of a series of measures to return to a selective system, including differential funding for grant-maintained schools, league tables, city technology colleges, later changed to specialist colleges with additional funding to enhance the specialist curriculum;
- significant increases in the number of children with English as their second language;
- changes in the management and integration of children with special needs into mainstream schools without appropriate funding and a significant increase in the numbers with statements of special educational need;
- the introduction of GCSE;
- the introduction of several versions of the National Curriculum;
- the introduction of standard assessment tests at ages 7, 11 and 14;
- the introduction of Ofsted inspections.

THE CAPPING OF EXPENDITURE

'Capping' (government restrictions on local authority expenditure) was a clever way of bringing a high-spending authority to its knees. It was slow but relentless, like medieval thumbscrews, making the ILEA appear to be harming children's education. For those of us trying to manage schools it was horrific. Ever since the ILEA was first capped in 1984, schools in London faced cuts in funding. This is bad for staff morale and it makes school leadership much more challenging. The ILEA had secured generous funding for education because it cared passionately for all children.

NATIONALLY SANCTIONED INDUSTRIAL ACTION BY TEACHERS, 1984–86

This cut off consultation between teachers, management, students and parents and regularly closed schools and impacted on children's learning. Headteachers in London were strongly in support of the teachers' right to a decent salary, but we were also determined to minimise the damage to children's education caused by the teachers' action. Hampstead School's NUT representative, George Matthews, worked hard to support the teachers' cause while remaining concerned not to harm the education of children. With the agreement of the majority of staff, parents and governors, we found a way of taking action, dramatic enough to make an impact, but which did not damage the children's learning. We proposed to the ILEA that we set up a continental day, teaching the children only in the morning. During this exciting time, we were to experience the value of an earlier start, more focused teaching and the release of significant time for both teachers and students during the afternoons. Neighbours no longer bothered by children at lunchtimes petitioned us to retain this arrangement. A slogan written on the school wall was 'I love the continental day'. It attracted a lot of publicity in support of teachers and creative educational change.

Sadly, with a more militant group enjoying the power of running Hampstead School NUT branch and posing serious challenges to the school leadership, there was a long period when it was difficult to move the school forward. The most serious problems occurred in early 1986 when the National Union of Teachers (NUT) and the National Association of Schoolmasters and Women Teachers (NASUWT) introduced staggered action. This meant that teachers walked out of lessons without warning for 20 minutes at a time. To communicate with staff I issued a daily bulletin, and to communicate with parents I held regular evening meetings – 'Open Doors' – which were well attended. I found the support of the parents a huge help during this very isolating period. To communicate with students, I was fortunate that, after I had called tutor group representatives to a meeting, they insisted that this became a whole-school council. I wanted to talk about making the school more attractive, because it was dirty, covered in graffiti and no teacher would put up displays of children's work. The students' interest was in having a school dinner!

In October 1985 the teachers had refused to do any lunch-time duties and the school had to close during the midday break, with no lunches being served. However, these were reinstated because the teachers felt guilty that the school-meals staff were not being paid and we obtained some financial help from the ILEA to pay for supervisory assistants. The students saw this as their victory and, to an extent, it was. It also provided another vital group to plan school developments. Considerable improvements in student management arose from the students' own code of conduct.

LONDON NATIONAL UNION OF TEACHERS UNOFFICIAL ACTION, 1986–89

The ILTA (Inner London Teachers Association) was very influential and determined to retain its considerable power. This was never controlled by either the national union or the ILEA, which meant that industrial action continued in London, with teachers withholding goodwill and refusing to cover for absent colleagues for much longer than in other parts of the country. On one day there were no teachers for any year 10 (14-15 years) classes, so I gave them an assembly for the whole morning. All 210 of them sat and listened to me talking about what I hoped we could achieve at the school. In order to get the year tutors into planning meetings together, I took each year group for a 70-minute assembly once a week.

From May 1987, the new regulations for the pay and conditions of teachers required staff to cover for absent colleagues. After several unofficial strikes, the union gave way.

THE LONDON IDENTIFICATION OF TEACHER EXERCISE

In 1987, the ILEA had a £100 million deficit. By drawing on reserves, this was reduced to £50 million, but this still meant that staffing had to be cut across the authority. Headteachers were required to produce curriculum plans to match reduced staffing levels and to select curriculum areas in which teachers could be identified as above authorised numbers. There is no doubt that a significant number of headteachers manipulated the system in order to identify weak and seriously failing teachers. Natural wastage would have been sufficient without the stigma, terror and massively lowered morale of both staff and heads.

Worse was to follow because, rather than make any teacher redundant, all schools were forced to take such identified teachers for any vacancies that occurred. This meant that staff were uprooted and, in some cases, seriously failing teachers were forced upon a school without having been through a selection procedure. The presence of such teachers undoubtedly contributed to poor standards in some schools. It was even more difficult because the ILEA did not appear to try – and the new unitary authorities took time – to acquire the expertise to manage competency procedures. The other serious problem that London schools faced was a staffing deficit so that all classes, even for practical subjects, contained at least 30 pupils and there were few support teachers for the increasing numbers with special needs.

I invited the senior inspector of HMI for London to visit Hampstead School and she decided that the situation was so grim that she would use the school as a case study. I even invited, probably unwisely, Sir Keith Joseph, who spent a day with us and agreed that the school was seriously understaffed. As the deposed Education Minister, he had no power, but it gave us wry satisfaction that he should see the result of his party's policies.

ABOLITION OF THE ILEA

The extent of Government determination to abolish the ILEA was made clear by the Secretary of State, Kenneth Baker: 'I vowed I would do everything I could to bring an end to an education authority where dogma took precedence over good education.' He was incensed that Marylebone Grammar School, a small selective school, had been closed (Ribbins and Sherratt, 1997, p. 93). This personal vendetta was perceived by all in the ILEA as being the major driving force for abolition. The Government claimed that the reason was central costs, policies on non-educational issues and tolerance of low standards, yet central costs increased ninefold after abolition. The issues on which the Government denigrated the ILEA were gender and race. On standards, the ILEA was more anxious than provincial LEAs to address issues of good teaching and learning, but London faced massive problems. The issue of raising expectations was a national one, stemming from a culture where, before 1939, only 5 per cent were considered academic and, from 1944 until the 1960s, a maximum of 20 per cent were selected for grammar schools. Even at Hampstead School up to 1985, only 30 per cent were considered to be academic enough to merit a place in the sixth form and only 17 per cent gained five GCE Ordinary level passes. (By 1997, the comparable figure had risen to 60 per cent.)

Fighting to retain the Inner London Education Authority took up a considerable amount of our time. One of the Hampstead School governors, Liz Williams, set up the All London Parents Action Group and we campaigned hard on behalf of London's children, but to no avail.

The abolition of the ILEA appeared to be part of the larger agenda of central control. Richard Aldrich (1996, p. 77) wrote that 'the control of education has been an issue throughout history' and quotes Lester Smith:

> For whoever exercises the supreme power in school affairs can determine educational thought and practice; and although this power may be shared or it may be united, it is as true of a school as it is of any other community that somewhere this governing authority must exist. (Lester Smith, 1945, p. 15)

The ILEA and many philanthropists had invested in resources and centres for London's children which were the envy of the world. They gave to the many who had nothing those extras which all good parents consider to be really important: holidays, experience of working with animals, support for the gifted in music, dance and drama, field centres for outdoor study and enjoyment of geography and biology. GCE Advanced-level English groups could study Wordsworth in the Lake District; vulnerable children from the Abbey Wood Estate on the Plumstead Marshes could enjoy walking and climbing in the Scottish Highlands.

There was wonderful support and provision for children who had identifiable special needs, in particular those who could not function in large inner-city schools. All this, like Beeching's axed railway networks, was lost. This was the most serious dismantling of provision for the underprivileged ever made. Now, with minimal resourcing from the small unitary authorities, these children drop out completely and form a significant and terrifying underclass whom we forget at our peril.

LOCAL AUTHORITY RELUCTANCE TO SUPPORT HEADTEACHERS

This has presented London heads with serious problems over the years. There are teachers who, for a variety of reasons, find themselves unable to cope, trapped in jobs they hate, facing children they cannot manage and who may do untold damage to the children entrusted to their care and to the colleagues who work alongside them. This situation cannot be left to fester. The teachers and support staff are the essence of any school and I have spent more time thinking about them, working with them, supporting and enabling them than on any other part of the job of headship. In order to deal with these difficult situations, there must be LEA support from the local inspectorate and from personnel departments with locally agreed procedures for both informal and formal stages of staff management. Training for governors is also critical. The ILEA had a policy of never sacking anyone; instead, teachers were moved into backwaters. I had one teacher who was never required to teach; his only function was to collect the papers and make the tea in the mathematics department office. Later, when I required him to teach, I eventually had to suspend him for pouring a kettle of water onto a student.

CHANGES TO THE PAY AND CONDITIONS OF SERVICE

Many London teachers had never attended meetings, contributed to whole-school events or worked with others since entering the profession. Some had lost the habit. In many cases teachers had become deskilled and deprofessionalised. It was essential that there was legislation to ensure that minimum professional duties were carried out. In 1987, I sent to all staff a paper on working time, covering the statutory 1,265 hours and other contractual duties. This mapped out what I could reasonably expect of colleagues, leaving plenty of time available for extra-curricular activities and attendance at evening meetings. I have never had to monitor the number of hours worked by teachers, although it might still be valuable to do so in order to give full recognition to their industry and dedication.

INTRODUCTION OF LOCAL MANAGEMENT OF SCHOOLS

London schools were given Additional Use of Resources money in 1973, which could be spent as the head and governors wished: to increase staffing, improve the site or increase the stock of books and equipment. As a result, London schools found LMS easy to implement. The main issue was, as always, managing with dwindling resources. Experience of spending our own money made us both more careful and more resourceful. In 1992, the London Residuary Body gave schools the money which had been frozen (an enforced school saving) and we used this over an extended period as a cushion for the time, which we foresaw, when resources would become scarcer. We were proved right, as the Conservative Government capped the London boroughs. The long-term planning of many schools was misinterpreted by both the LEA and the Government, which believed that schools were being too generously resourced, as they appeared to be sitting on large reserves. The additional money had allowed us to plan budgets on a longer-term basis, which is what all schools should be able to do. It is not sensible to run a £3 million a year business without being able to make financial projections beyond a single year.

Hampstead School has never been persuaded to opt out, although two schools in Camden with religious foundations obtained grant-maintained status. We have always considered that it was essential for all schools to be answerable to locally elected representatives. However, we have become more critical and more demanding of quality at the local level. Financial cuts have severely affected the ability of the small LEA to deliver a high quality service. Many have destroyed central services to protect their schools.

MEASURES TO RETURN TO A SELECTIVE SYSTEM

Measures to increase selection have always incensed me as ways of rejecting the many for the sake of the few. Covert selection has always taken place in London schools and is present in our two local voluntary-aided schools and in the church schools, which have control over their selection process. They have all had their own strategies, such as taking in a proportion of musically gifted pupils, to ensure that they gained more than their share of the brighter children. Church schools have always interviewed families applying. With only two local grant-maintained schools which had always selected, Hampstead School has at least been spared the more overt forms of selection in other schools which add to the hierarchies and make parents anxious and angry. The 'haves' in such a system do not only affect themselves, but have an impact on all local schools and their intakes. The impact at the 11-plus stage is well documented, if conveniently forgotten, and cannot be the way forward.

Another anomaly in the Camden area is the presence of more girls' schools. In Camden there are 23 more forms of entry for girls than boys, which creates a serious imbalance in the mixed schools. Taking children from the immediate area creates a 45/55 split between boys and girls; in other local schools this is as much as 20/80.

I have always valued knowing where we are in relation to the performance of other schools at both local and national levels. But this is a professional interest and crude league tables are easily misinterpreted if they are taken out of context. I am aware of the serious impact such tables make on recruitment and this was a major factor in closing one school and in threatening another in Camden. Polarisation seems inevitable.

INCREASES IN NUMBER OF CHILDREN WITH ENGLISHVAS A SECOND LANGUAGE

Hampstead School, like many in London, has become an international school, with children speaking over 80 different home languages and dialects. There has also been a large increase in young people seeking asylum, a significant number of whom are unaccompanied minors. We have nearly 150 such children. We became so concerned about the plight of these children that a group of staff and students, led by Athy Demetriades, set up a charity, Children of the Storm, which raises significant amounts of money to support these remarkable young people, who have often been through the most harrowing of experiences. The children have contributed much to schools in London, as they have valued the English education system and the freedom of society. Camden LEA has recognised this group and has resourced both a borough coordinator and post-holders in those schools with significant numbers of refugees. There have been many fights with the Government in trying to secure the position of individual children.

Supporting children with English as their second language has to be a whole-school concern, using specialist teachers in the same way as special needs teachers. It also requires languages to be taught in a broader way so that all children moving towards bilingualism are able to gain accreditation in their home language. We have set up special events to recognise and celebrate, as well as support, groups from different backgrounds. This need was never fully recognised by the Conservative Government.

INTEGRATION OF CHILDREN WITH SPECIAL NEEDS INTO MAINSTREAM SCHOOLS

While the ILEA was providing education for London schools, children who could not manage the mainstream, the ones who now drop out of school, all had caring centres where many were nurtured back into society. As a head of year at Pimlico School, I looked after a year cohort of 300 children. Nearly one-third of these had some form of special need, many with emotional and behavioural problems that appeared to be linked to inadequate parenting or serious deprivation. Child abuse was only just being recognised. Because of the wealth of high-quality external support only one of these children had to be permanently excluded during their time at the school. The rest went to centres, such as Interaction, a drama support group, or the Finsbury Unit, both of which were highly successful. Other children were well supported for part of the time by an on-site unit run by a 'saintly' man who was amazingly tolerant and who rescued many.

Currently, we have capped funding to cope with increasing special needs. At Hampstead School we have chosen to have a 'Rolls-Royce provision' with individual support teachers who play an important role in advising class teachers on good strategies for managing the learning and support of all children. This has meant that fewer children have had to progress towards a statement of special educational needs because they can be supported by the classroom teachers. Other schools had chosen to use less expensive staff with no teaching experience. As an extra person in the classroom, these adults are helpful, but they cannot make much of an input. Because of recent severe financial constraints, Hampstead School will now have to do the same. Special needs support funding is having to be rationed by political imperatives rather than being led by student need.

INTRODUCTION OF THE GENERAL CERTIFICATE OF SECONDARY EDUCATION (GCSE)

This was ideal: an integrated examination for all students who were to have a broad, balanced core curriculum until the age of 16. A major concern of mine was the poor performance of girls. GCSEs helped girls to achieve and meant that students could not get away with selective mugging up just before examinations. With coursework, they had to work for the whole two years. They also had to carry out several pieces of extended work. However, the subsequent reductions in the coursework components do not help girls or students who find formal examinations intimidating.

INTRODUCTION OF SEVERAL VERSIONS OF THE NATIONAL CURRICULUM

This has been another powerful lever for change, which we have welcomed, particularly as it prevents the appalling sex-stereotypical choices students used to make at the age of 13. However, the introduction of the National Curriculum was too hasty and this meant that we wasted scarce finance on textbooks which soon became obsolete. We could ill afford such waste. However, we have always agreed that children should be entitled to a broad and balanced core of knowledge, skills and areas of understanding which equip them for the future. The introduction of technology and broad and balanced science, which we had been recommending to bright students for many years, was very welcome and we had the teams of staff ready to deliver. We had also been successful in gaining Technology Schools Initiative funding in 1992 and we were awarded another tranche through the Technology College Funding in 1997, as one of the first given by the new Labour Government. Our major complaints with the National Curriculum have been that it is overloaded with content, that it is heavily subject-based and that everything seems to need assessing! If content could be massively reduced, then key stage 3 could be condensed into two years. This would help children to maintain their enthusiasm and would mean that key stage 4 could become a much broader and more exciting set of integrated courses, thus ensuring that students really obtain a flavour of the whole curriculum. Specialisms should be a thing of the past. Valerie Bayliss proposes that education should be built around information and communications technology, thus ensuring that new key competencies for life are developed (Bayliss, 1998). This can happen only if curriculum content is drastically reduced.

INTRODUCTION OF STANDARD ASSESSMENT TESTS

Hurried legislation never works well and the last Conservative Government was so keen to 'name and shame' underperforming schools that they failed to allow sufficient preparation time for the new tests, which were not properly piloted and checked to ensure validity. Teachers are generally a most law-abiding group of people and this made them into lawbreakers overnight. Once you have disobeyed one set of instructions with impunity it becomes easier to do so again!

INTRODUCTION OF OFSTED INSPECTIONS

Hampstead School's Ofsted inspection took place in May 1996 and we were given a good report. Our group of inspectors was a strange mixture, assembled by a large consortium which had put in the cheapest bid. It is important to be publicly accountable and to know broadly how we perform in comparison with other schools, but Ofsted should exercise greater quality control over its teams. The Ofsted team was criticised by our parents for being all white and Anglo-Saxon! Very few of them had experience of inner-city schools.

MOVING FORWARD

Now that we have a Government determined to put resources into education and to make it a high-status activity we have a wonderful opportunity to improve inner-city education in London. What is needed in order to achieve this is some creative thinking and action.

PREVENTING THE UNDERCLASS

A London Regional Group should be funded nationally to coordinate, research and evaluate: identification criteria; best practice in assessment; managing children with specific special needs, emotional and anti-social behaviour problems; the teaching of key skills; establishing independent learning patterns; the use of ICT; alternatives to exclusion; and multi-agency family support.

DEVELOPMENTS IN THE USE OF INFORMATION AND COMMUNICATIONS ACROSS THE CURRICULUM

My brilliant director of new technologies and independent learning at

Hampstead School, Phil Taylor, has described the steps we need to take in order to become both creative and proactive in the use of technology. He describes the first step as being able to turn on the computer, where we are very much prescribed by the machine. We then use programs such as word processing and spreadsheets, followed by data logging and creative packages such as Publisher and Computer Aided Design. Finally, we are able to mould the machines to our own requirements and write our own programs. How many teachers can write programs? Not many, but most pupils have no fear of being able to master machines. It is essential that all teachers have their own computer and are given training so that they can take full advantage of new technologies and communications links. Technical support has to be provided, even in tight staffing situations, in every school. As a motivator and supporter of learning for London's inner-city children, it is outstanding, making young and old into independent learners and opening up a world of increasing wonders, contacts and excitement.

HIGH-QUALITY TEACHER RECRUITMENT

The Teacher Training Agency (TTA) has asked schools to help to recruit people to the teaching profession. Teachers should not be daunted, but excited, by this. The TTA itself cannot recruit. It is too remote. It may well be important to target people in their early thirties who have never thought of teaching. We could use industry and business links to give people a taste of belonging to exciting groups of people who are doing one of the most important jobs in the world. We need to show people that teaching is enjoyable and give them the support to train in a developing field. We also need to ensure that teachers are not too exhausted, and that they are well resourced and well paid.

DEVELOPMENT AND TRAINING TIME

In order to create more time in the school day, the pattern used in independent schools could be considered: an early start, a full morning and then a range of different activities during the afternoons, flexible enough to free teams of staff for training, preparation and development. This would do much to restore professional self-confidence.

At Hampstead School, we currently use twilight sessions for a school-based Masters Degree, taught by the Institute of Education's International

School Effectiveness Unit: 15 colleagues are enjoying this. We want to build this in as an integral biannual opportunity. This still leaves a fourth evening session where teachers should be able to have some recreation and important family time. After-school activities for children would then be an integrated part of the school day and could support children who have difficulties with independent study or who need extension opportunities. There could be joint learning sessions in ICT for teachers and students.

TEACHER–RESEARCHER–IMPLEMENTERS

Teachers are well placed to examine and rigorously evaluate what is going on in the classroom. The TTA is supporting research projects to improve pedagogy. There are so many important areas to develop using in-house researchers who can then implement valid improved pedagogy: assessment, managing differentiation, uses for ICT, transferable skills, multi-disciplinary approaches and citizenship competencies. These could be disseminated using the Internet and the Government's National Grid for Learning.

CURRICULUM CHANGE

My earlier proposal to start key stage 4 one year earlier would enable schools to offer, for example, Crest Awards, the Duke of Edinburgh Award, the Youth Award Scheme and community projects, which would be exciting for both students and teachers. This would require a considerable reduction in content in the National Curriculum, which has grown at a time when knowledge retention is less important than knowledge manipulation. Those who advise on the reduction of the National Curriculum remind me of those occasions when I try to reduce the number of books in my house. I spend hours looking at them and eventually, reluctantly, find one duplicate that I can part with.

DEVELOPING GOOD LEARNING ENVIRONMENTS

If we want young people to value and respect the environment and to appreciate beauty and design, and if we want them to value their own finished pieces of work and those of others, then we need to create learning environments that are truly outstanding. Croydon's wonderful new library is a learning centre for all ages. It is the most exciting architectural design, packed with beautiful and enjoyable sculpture and paintings; it has many books and much technology; it is warm, quiet and carpeted and has places for people to work, reflect and eat. If I could steal it and make it the centrepiece of a new school I would do so. Perhaps, by recognising and valuing young people more, their territorial graffiti would seem less important to them and we might prevent the destructive vandalism.

Schools need good assembly areas, lecture facilities, multi-purpose teaching spaces and plenty of technical support. High-quality teaching in such a learning environment would be the envy of the rest of the world.

9

FOLLOWING THE THIRD WAY? TEACHERS AND NEW LABOUR

MARTIN LAWN

INTRODUCTION

Although the original title for this chapter was 'The Teaching Profession', I believe it is no longer possible to use this term confidently. After the radical changes, continuing in the present, in the government of education, it is no longer possible to stretch the term to cover the shifts in meaning and the new practices of work associated with teachers. To speak of the 'teaching profession' is to speak the language of the past in England. The ideas and practices upon which the great post-war education system was built have been thoroughly demolished so that, in effect, a new vocabulary now has to be used to explain the purposes and practices of teaching. This is a political issue in that the new Labour Government has a limited but useful capacity to create a progressive alternative to this key idea of the past: however, the ability of a nation state, especially a trading nation like England, to create a version of its teachers which is separate from other kinds of employees, at home or abroad, is severely curtailed today. The specific meaning given to the term 'teaching profession' in England was created, sustained and eventually eroded because it was a product of a time, of a particular social and political period. The language hovers around still but the conditions which sustained it have gone.

The post-war ideals of public service were deeply bound up with descriptions of the growth and development of education in England. In common with other public sector work, in the civil service, local government, health service and so on, the idea of public service has operated as a key descriptor of the responsibilities and practices of work and client relations. Teacher professionalism was broadly associated with the rise of the public service of education and it was most clearly seen within the post-war education service where teachers were 'viewed' as constituting a collective partner with the local and national government of education. Teacher professionalism and public service were closely entwined and symbiotically related. The decline of a public sector, in terms of employment strength, owing to the use of agencies or private companies or to its marketisation (so that in practice it is difficult to recognise a *distinctive* public sector practice and ethos), has led to the decline in the sector which, amongst other things, gave teacher professionalism its use value. The practical disappearance of the discourse of professionalism, previously used by government and by teacher associations and by many other education participants, is significant; it is the end of an empowering language for teachers.

In this chapter, I want to look at the public service context in which teacher professionalism grew; the way in which the marketisation of education, and the political context which sustained it, has altered the situation; and finally the possibilities for a resurrection of a new public domain into which teachers could fit.

THE MAKING OF THE PUBLIC PROFESSIONAL

In the 1920s, new ideas about a public sector and its administration were being created and thinkers associated with the young Labour Party described the future education system. For example, Sydney Webb, the Fabian thinker, had recently described the relation between a new government function of a 'systematic education' and the large number of teachers required to work in it: he wrote about the special knowledge of teachers and their claim to 'exercise a professional judgement, to formulate distinctive opinions upon its own and upon cognate services, and to enjoy its own appropriate share in the corporate government of its own working life' (Webb, 1918, p. 3).

The idea of teachers' taking 'an increased measure of corporate responsibility' for the running of the service (partly to mitigate a state bureaucracy) came to fruition in the immediate post-war period. Webb was arguing for the co-optation by the state of a large and growing group of workers who had to be turned away from working for the rich and powerful and towards 'the entire community':

> it is the duty of each profession to take the needs of the whole community for its sphere . . . it must claim as its function the provision of its

> distinctive service wherever this is required, irrespective of the affluence or status of the persons in need . . . it must emphatically not regard itself as hired for the service only of those who pay fees and it must insist therefore on being accorded by public authority and where necessary at the public expense, the opportunity and the organisation that will enable this full professional service being rendered wherever it is required. (Webb, 1918, p. 8)

There was an assumption, common to other forms of work (within the ideas of the time, of guild socialism and syndicalism), that all employees should have a recognised stake in their work, its organisation and its management. The post-war arrival of the Labour Government in 1945 was accompanied by an urgent need to rebuild the schools (with a scarcity of resources), the implementation of a new Education Act with a profound shortage of teachers, and the creation of the welfare system, which incorporated education within the distribution of benefits. It is this association with the emerging welfare services which probably affected teachers' work the most, not only with its prevailing sense of public service (now consolidated into this version of the administration of public services within a welfare society) but with an emphasis on universalism and equality of opportunity.

The period from the 1950s to the early 1970s has been described as an era of social democracy in which many public organisations were shaped by 'the mantle of professionalism' (Burns, 1977). Such was the dominance of professionals and their values in the post-war period that Perkin [1989] has called it the high point in an 'age of professionalism' (Ranson and Stewart, 1994, p. 45).

In the post-war period, progressivism of different kinds was closely linked with, even congruent with, a pervasive ideology of Englishness in which the natural democratic values of England were compared with the authoritarian regimes of Europe (Alexander, 1954). This gradual correlation between professionalism, a mass schooling, welfare and reconstructionist ideologies and the making of a democratic society acknowledged the crucial position of teachers: as heroes of reconstruction, as pedagogic innovators, as carers, as partners of and within the public. This policy gave meaning to teaching. In the 1950s, teachers were praised as the bedrock of the new welfare society, as the founders of the reconstruction of the education system and as the guardians of the citizenry of the future. Teachers were professionals, fostered by the state, partners in the deliberations of policy, able to influence the direction and control of the system. In effect, they were leaders and followers, circulating within the service through its administration, democratic government and associations, as classroom teachers, representatives, governors and advisers.

So powerful is this language, and that period, that it is still used as the key way to explain the past and to analyse the present: yet this period, its assumptions about education and public service, its administrative structures and its closed national boundaries is no longer in place.

This is not to argue that the system was perfect or even that it worked properly. Indeed, there was a real gap between the actual power teachers wielded in the school and the power they appeared to wield in society. This same system was characterised by bureaucracy, inflexibility and local dogmatism. It seems clear that most primary schools were extremely quiescent and compliant towards their local education authority in the period 1950s–70s. The duty of the school was to work quietly and wait for instructions. Its teachers had a lot of influence over the work of the classroom (curriculum, books, style of teaching, pupil organisations and so on) and none over the school organisation and policy, but they existed within a school system which officially and continually referred to them as partners, consulted with their elected representatives and assumed that the teacher was a highly skilled and responsible professional. Teachers were trusted and they participated in the organisation, strategy and development of education at the local and national level.

RESTRUCTURING WORK

In the late 1990s this national system of values and relations has been dismantled, partially from within and also from without. These changes have many roots – deindustrialisation, fiscal crises, postmodernity, ideological conflict, cultural issues – but the driving forces in English schools have been the marketisation of the public services, the centralisation of power by Government and its agencies, the loss of confidence in national identity and economic competitiveness. Disguising itself as a revived modernisation of schooling towards effectiveness and improvement, the schooling system has been radically reconstructed. It is not just in the daily work of teachers in which changes can be seen; it is in the lack of a supportive national debate about them; they exist within a form of punitive corporation, focused entirely on competition and output. Their national role has disappeared and they are either deskilled or multiskilled employees of local sites of work, working to regulation and assessment.

The changes in the school system are not confined to education alone; they are part of the shift in organisation and work taking place across the public sector. In a recent discussion of the restructuring of work generally and in the public sector (Lash and Urry, 1994), the limits of technical change in people-intensive industries, the reorganisation of the production processes (including the intensification of work at lower levels) and the limits of product transformation in a public service were seen as the most pertinent to schooling. Education cannot begin to make a different kind of product or produce it elsewhere in the world; nor can it overcome its reliance on people (rather than technology). But, the main forms of restructuring in this sector, it was suggested, will be through the intensification, commodification, concentration and domesticisation of work. People in the public sector will be managed more intensively; a variety of attempts will be made to 'mimic' markets; larger units of production and administration will be created with more powerful managers; the quality of state-trained labour will decrease; and there will be a rise in the supply of unpaid or voluntary labour. There is evidence that each of these categories of restructuring is at work in teaching and its management through the rise of private companies (providing inspection, consultancy, financial controls, specialist services and resources and so on), the sharp climb in the number of teaching assistants and new agencies providing teachers for schools. So, in a broad way, it is possible to refer generally to intensification or domesticisation in relation to schooling.

It is not just that the work has changed structurally. Teaching is now redefined as a form of flexible and reskilled competence-based labour; teachers operate a regulated curriculum and internal assessment system in a decentralised external school market. Because of the emphasis on controlling teachers and their work, trying to alter radically their skills and regulate their performance, and denying them power over the content of their work, the restructuring of teaching has tended to be punitive in tone in England. The restructuring and redesign of teaching in England has some of the same features but not the same tone as it has in many US (and European) locations, where it is closely connected to school reform. Consequently, current English work on school improvement tends to see the redesign of teaching and of the institution as an operational by-product of policy reforms and there seems to be little comparison of the change in tone between England and its fellow states. The constant references to change and improvement, and to the 'high' percentage of 'failing' teachers (especially from Her Majesty's Chief Inspector of Schools) distinguishes this English tradition. The final Conservative version of teaching, contained within a model in which individual responsibility and incentive reward were the key features, seems to be intact within the New Labour philosophy.

Schools exist within a market for education and they have to pay for some of their activities by raising finance through selling services or attracting sponsorship or saving money. Increasingly, the managers of the school employ learning assistants who are cheaper than teachers although less skilled, or they view the fixed costs of the teaching force as increasingly open to manipulation. Teachers exist within the realm of powerful regulatory bodies, such as Ofsted, and a local education authority, which generate statistics about their work based on every conceivable quantitative piece of data, and then place schools (and increasingly their teachers) into national categories. They exist within a visionary school improvement policy field so every national and local regulation or initiative, likely sponsor, local adviser or private consultant, many of their school managers, local in-service courses and special improvement schemes (such as Investors in People) are focused on improvements to all aspects of the school but especially the work of the teachers and the quality of the school management.

Increasingly, the reform of schooling has depended on tight stipulations about teachers' work. Curriculum and assessment regulations have been reduced in scope, but schools are inspected on the basis of a tight specification of teacher competence, budgetary expertise, curriculum and managerial competencies and parental evaluations. The Teacher Training Agency has produced lists of teacher competencies and a grading of the profession into a hierarchy of skill-bearers, including a professional qualification for headteachers focused on leadership skills of motivation and management. In addition, a policy of 'zero tolerance' in the dismissal of 'incompetent' teachers, new appraisal agreements for teachers, a new grade of advanced skills teacher and a national curriculum in primary English and mathematics in teacher education have been instituted.

All this is distinguishing the new English Way. Threats and regulation define the English system as once did praise and a language of partnership. Indeed, in a way that is quite ironic, it is now seen within Europe as another sign of the strange perversions of an Englishness which once, of course, defined itself against the authoritarianism and anti-democratic systems prevalent in Europe. Professionalism, leadership and the state were bound together and it is the breaking down and radical removal of this relationship which has caused a crisis in the meaning of work in teaching which is greater than the crisis about how to regulate or improve or compete or manage. While it is possible to make teachers work more effectively, this might be at the expense of motivation, control and responsibility.

LOSING OUT AND FRAGMENTATION

The language of individual success and responsibility is the common language of work today, and there is no distinction between teaching and other forms of work, including the private, commercial and public sectors. As the teachers have had little recourse to a positive image of teaching and a popular image of public service, they have had either to leave teaching or observe some form of loyalty to schooling.

In addition to the shift out of teaching, teachers have had to recognise openly that the idea of 'losing out' is available to them in teaching (officially and not just unofficially as before) and secondly, that being a teacher is no longer a category recognisable through its qualification level (and that an increase in 'unskilled or semi-skilled' teachers is taking place). Firstly, groups of teachers will lose out in the market (and so in the restructuring) just as others will make gains. There is a legitimate expectation that current inequalities in teaching will continue as local management of schools (LMS) produces a differentiation of the work-force as much as a practice of collegiality. In that process of differentiation, a disproportionate percentage of women teachers and black teachers will continue to lose out in pay, promotion or recruitment. They will lose out in the secondary schools because men in shortage subjects obtain responsibility allowances and in the primary schools, where they predominate, because there are fewer such allowances. A 1991 survey reported that teachers were mentally retreating into the classroom: 'These teachers reported a pervasive sense of bewilderment and frustration at a system which did not, as they saw it, recognise their virtues, reward their efforts or offer any help with their future career' (*Times Educational Supplement*, 12 October 1991).

The second aspect of LMS is the new emphasis on workforce pliability. The idea of a skilled teacher was closely related to the idea of a graduate or certificated teacher profession in the recent past, and often in opposition to the employment of new routes for the unskilled or semi-skilled teacher. It was easier to fight for a graduate profession during the post-war project of an improving education service but it will not be so easy in a service fragmented and marked by inequality. An Audit Commission report on LMS in the primary sector (1991) emphasises this idea of a differentiated workforce in a new way. Expressing it quite bluntly at one point, the Commission argues that with a fixed budget, school governors might decide to employ (unskilled/semi-skilled) classroom assistants and not teachers: 'at least two classroom assistants might be employed full-time for the cost of one teacher' (Audit

Commission, 1991, p. 32). Indeed, the whole emphasis of the report appears to be on the 'flexible delivery' of primary education by the use of untrained labour. The word 'delegate' begins to take on a new aspect in this version of LMS. School governors (through their teachers) 'delegate' tasks to untrained assistants in the schools. They will delegate (to 'less qualified but capable' classroom assistants) the routine work and supervision of some pupil tasks and they will use classroom assistants to prepare materials for lessons and work with small groups of children.

Professional expertise, in line with HMI thinking, is increasingly defined as a supervisory skill (an unwritten aspect of restructuring skills) and it will be used to supervise semi-skilled or unskilled workers in the classroom. These people will be 'locally available' and suitable to be recruited as teachers ('licensed and articled teachers') and as classroom assistants. Their employment (the cost of it compared to 'real' teachers) will depend upon the amount of (free) parental cooperation within the school (Audit Commission, 1991, p. 33). The labour market for teachers will be affected by local conditions of employment and their own employment, scale and discretionary payments will be judged, in part, against the cost of employing local untrained or partly-trained labour. Recent publications by HMI and by a DfEE-commissioned project have emphasised the new roles in schools for non-teaching staff (Department for Education, 1992; Mortimore *et al.*, 1993). Since 1989, the number of full-time equivalent classroom assistants in schools has nearly doubled from 48,000 to nearly 80,000. With other school support staff, they now comprise 14 per cent of the primary school budget.

THE THIRD WAY: A NEW ROAD FOR TEACHERS?

The political context, in which the new Labour Government is a defining factor, contains an educational direction, focusing on modernising the system and improving schools, around which the older structures of agency and punitive discourse are still prevalent. Encouragement and discipline are the watchwords; individual responsibility is the defining concept; regulation and flexible financial rewards are the ways of management. The paradox is that this new radical direction is dependent upon old-fashioned structural control. Centralised blueprints and prescriptions are not an efficient approach to change, do not enrol people or allow them to 'mimic' social movements; nor do they recognise the limitations of government knowledge. In addition, it is a strange contrast with the 1940s and 1950s in which professional partnership and responsibility allowed local education authorities and teachers to participate in the service, to a greater or lesser degree.

There seem to be two problems here. Firstly, what idea of participation and social change is available to harness teachers again to the task of aiding the creation of a good and effective society? Secondly, what equivalent motivating movement is available to teachers and their managers in their daily work?

'Stakeholding' is the idea which informs the approach of New Labour to social policy. At its simplest, stakeholding is an interest in ensuring that every citizen has a stake in society and a voice in the way it is run and that, at the level of work organisations, all are able to participate in the making of decisions. A key feature of this new direction is a strong belief in individual responsibility and wider democratic participation in government. This is a unifying approach, to be used across the range of public and private organisations which will deliver public policy. It appears to have the potential to be the late-twentieth century equivalent of the mid-twentieth century democracy and citizenship movement in which teaching was viewed as a key part. It would involve the re-establishment of a public domain which had been reduced to a series of moral duties, combined with punitive action.

I have previously tried to compare the way that the restructuring of teaching has been managed in the USA and England (Lawn, 1995). In the recent past, while England was able to develop strong discursive and hugely important myths, like 'professional power', to describe its education service, the USA appeared to devise educational solutions based on the idea of 'teacher proofing' the school and curriculum, an anti-professional perspective. In the late 1990s, in the USA, school reform seems to be a reaction to the history of these bureaucratising tendencies in educational management and employment, reproducing a centre/periphery division between administrators, curriculum experts and teachers. The American history of extensive controls in education, built on to minimum conditions of employment, was based on the premise that the teacher was a barrier to change and efficiency. The new reforms appear to be trying to reverse this situation. Perhaps this is due to the loss of confidence in these peculiar ways of managing organisations and production (in a time of economic recession) when faced with successful competitors using quite different approaches. If production and quality cannot be raised by specification, assessment and bureaucracy, then teamwork, professional accountability and decentralisation might work. However, unlike parts of the USA, in England there may be a move towards teamwork, but within an increasingly harsh national system which does not spend time praising teachers or reiterating their professional value but, instead, concentrates on producing school and teacher effectiveness targets and new forms of regulation or specification about teaching.

Most of all, compared with the past and elsewhere (in the USA or Europe), there is the complete lack of an official production of a positive view of the teacher. If the past was a Teaching Society, today is a Learning Society. The positive statements from the DfEE, Labour Party and Teacher Training Agency are about learners, not teachers. Teachers are to be controlled and their work evaluated by reference to learning targets set for others; their effectiveness is judged according to how these targets of recruitment or success are met. Of course, as these targets shift, so will the control deepen; this can be seen clearly in the increasing demands on schools through Ofsted, especially on the supervision time and leadership offered to other teachers and the constant references to 'failing' teachers.

The new Government has tried to make the agenda of school improvement its overriding aim, but within a basically intact penalising system. The problem for the Government is that it is unable to establish the old professional partnership. It needs to motivate its teachers but it has been able only to develop technologies of control. To be fair, the new Government associates its idea of a General Teaching Council (GTC) with a restoration of 'teachers' professional pride' (DfEE Press Release, 31 August 1997). However, it is an extremely weak version of a council and occasional references to professional pride sit uneasily with the carping and bullying statements that issue from Ofsted and with the lack of power in the GTC. The creation of a category of advanced skills teachers in schools seems to be a sign of weakness not of strength and, if anything, implies a differentiated professional language and cadre in teaching. Even a professionalism described as a responsibility to improve the school, a much reduced version of its former self, still needs a national perspective and it would have to counter the current official line which sees teachers as under-effective employees. This circle cannot be squared at present; and the problem will surely be exacerbated by the introduction of performance-related pay for teachers.

Professionalism in teaching appears to be a matter of working effectively in any way the teacher is commanded to, using the skills validated and prescribed by the Government and its agencies. While this might be unambiguous, it barely motivates. To be able to do all that is required, even though this constantly changes, might be a source of some satisfaction but it leaves the teacher as no more than an efficient employee.

The overriding educational policy objectives of this new Government are, at first sight, admirable – raising standards for all, tackling underachievement and improving pupil performance – and so is the statement that it will be the skill and dedication of teachers which will deliver these objectives. But regulation and threatening behaviour seem to be short of the mark in their capacity to engineer a positive response from teachers. It was impossible for the last Conservative Government to associate the shortage of teachers or low teacher morale with the radical reforms they had pushed through. What would be intolerable would be a similar response from the new Government, even though it has goodwill on its side and very worthwhile aims to fulfil. What it has not yet achieved is any evidence of a new strategy for its teachers. A move to the idea of stakeholding would legitimate the new practices of teaching in schools as other than intensified managerialism. It would be the way in which a renewal of meaning and purpose in teaching might be achieved.

In new forms of work an emphasis on the culture and meaning of work in organisations is being created. The crisis of work today is in the social aspects of work, not in its skill, technology or the market. Work organisations have to create for their employees a simulated community of work, replacing older competitive cultures (the professional association or expert group), denying conflict and alienation, and harnessing energies and skills in new ways. Working in the team or the family must replace isolated work and work ideas based on private knowledge and attitudes of conflict. Work is then intimately connected to others, in the family team, through mutual obligations which are stronger than supervisor/employee relations. These relations of work have to be created by a leadership (individual or group); this generates a culture of work in which new ties of solidarity try to make the production work and the organisation succeed. In schools, this can be produced through group endeavour but, without a national discourse in which praise and reward, purpose and commitment, meaning and discussion, evidence and analysis are manifest, this will not generate a new form of teacher, teaching and association.

A combination of stakeholding and a freedom (and responsibility) to make meaning in work would radically alter the current situation in England. It is unlikely that the regulatory devices will disappear (and perhaps they should not) but the climate of work, the engagement of purpose, the re-creation of meaning would be able to counterbalance the insistent managerial return to limited notions of product quality and improvement targets.

10

INSPECTION: FROM HMI TO OFSTED

JOHN DUNFORD

PROFESSIONAL INDEPENDENCE

Since 1839, Her/His Majesty's Inspectorate (HMI) has inspected schools in England and Wales and has held a unique position within the education system. Although based in the Education Department for most of this time, HMI retained a high degree of professional independence, established in the nineteenth century and jealously guarded against interference from Government ministers. A House of Commons select committee in 1968 and a succession of committees of inquiry and internal departmental reviews upheld the independence of HMI and attested to its value within the education system.

From the school perspective in 1979, the inspectorate was seen as an authoritative voice on education policy and on pedagogy, especially in primary schools where inspectors tended to be more didactic in their advice. The inspectors themselves were regarded as senior professionals, bringing into schools a breadth of experience impossible for an individual schoolteacher to obtain. To the classroom teacher the inspector was a distant, and sometimes overbearing, figure and some inspectors went beyond the authoritative to the authoritarian. Teachers criticised them for their remoteness from the classroom, especially where the inspector had not taught in a state school. For teachers in deprived areas, the gap between their experience and that of a visiting inspector was even wider. The best inspectors made their judgements on the basis of what they saw, in the context in which it was taking place; the worst came into school with a predetermined view of how a subject should be taught to a particular age group and judged the teaching only against that narrow set of assumptions. Inevitably, in an inspectorate of around 450, there were many inspectors of both types, but the overall view of the teaching profession was that HMI was greatly to be valued and its professional independence was regarded as an important bulwark against the state.

TYPES OF INSPECTION

School inspections varied from a one-day visit by a single inspector to a week-long full inspection of a large school by about 20 inspectors. The majority of visits fell into the first category and the day always ended with an account of the inspector's findings to the headteacher. Such visits took place for a number of reasons, but were usually part of an HMI national survey of a particular subject or aspect of education. The short inspection of a secondary school led to a report on general aspects of the school, but did not usually include comments on individual subjects. The full inspection covered every aspect of the work of the school and resulted in an extensive report, including sections on each subject area.

For a full inspection, the team was led by the reporting inspector (RI), who notified the school only about four weeks in advance, although the period of notice was sometimes shorter and gave very little time to prepare the large amount of documentation which was required by the school. Certainly there was no time to rewrite an inadequate scheme of work or apply a coat of paint to an unsightly building. From the perspective of the teachers in the school, this was a stressful time. Most of them experienced a full inspection only once during their professional careers and they knew little of what to expect, apart from an inspector sitting in the corner of their classroom, probably more than once during the week, and observing the quality of the teaching.

From the head's viewpoint, the period before the inspection week was crucial. The teaching staff wanted to know 'Why us?', a question which the head would have discussed with the RI during a preliminary visit. Since very few, if any, of the staff had experienced an inspection, many also wanted to know how the inspectors would operate and what they would want to see. The best answer to the final part of that question was 'everything' – classroom displays, toilet walls, resources, assembly, tutor periods, the lunch break, times of arrival at school and lessons, as well as the more obvious matters such as teaching styles, pupil responses and relationships with the community outside the school. The inspection was not an appraisal of individual teachers, but of teaching and learning, although it was difficult to convince teachers that it was not they who were on trial.

The RI offered to talk to the teaching staff before the inspection and it was a brave head who declined this offer. Some inspectors were good at putting the staff at ease in these talks, but others left the staff in a greater state of stress than they found them. The result was that teachers often gave 'safe' lessons during the week and many inspection reports thus commented on dull and unimaginative teaching by people capable of giving the most exciting lessons.

The style of a full inspection changed little during the post-war years and it was surprising that other models were not adopted by HMI. It is often said that an inspection provides a snapshot of a school at a particular moment, but snapshots lack depth and, although the antennae of experienced inspectors were able to assess rapidly the standards of education in a school, the inspectors often failed to put the work of the school into the context of the community which it served. Part of the reason for this was that full inspections, as originally intended, were led by a locally based inspector, the general inspector, who knew the schools in the area well. The general inspector was able to place the findings of the visiting inspectors into the context of a detailed knowledge of the school and the local community, thus ensuring that the snapshot was in focus. By 1979, the role of the general inspector had diminished – and was to disappear altogether during the early 1980s – as HMI extended its work into so many areas other than school inspection. The national role of HMI collectively had replaced the local knowledge of inspectors individually. In fact, there was little criticism at the time of the process of inspection, apart from the speed of judgement and the feeling that the advice offered by inspectors was sometimes out of touch with the reality of the local school situation.

INSPECTION REPORTS

At the end of an inspection, of whatever length or type, there would be a verbal report to the head of department or class teacher and then to the head. From 1990–91, the chair of governors was invited to be present for the report to the head. Because of the speed and intensity of these reports, and because there had often been little discussion between the inspector and the head during the week of a full inspection, it was difficult for the head to take in all the detail of the report and simultaneously to correct any errors. For a short or a full inspection, a verbal report would subsequently be given by the RI to the governing body, whose members had the opportunity to ask questions and discuss the findings. The final report would be produced several weeks – or even months – later.

In 1983, the then Secretary of State, Sir Keith Joseph, decided that school inspection reports should be published. He was an avid reader of such reports and believed that publication – an early manifestation of the 'naming and shaming' policy of the 1997 Labour Government – would contribute to the spreading of good practice and would give parents important additional information about schools. Inspection reports contained no surprises for the school, which had already received the findings orally. Written comments were often toned down in comparison with the verbal report to the head. The 'outstanding' features of a school became merely 'successful' and boring lessons were reported as 'lacking pace'. This dilution of the inspectors' conclusions was not always helpful to a headteacher who was trying to reform an underperforming subject department. It was, however, welcomed after 1983 when poor reports would nearly always result in extensive criticism in the local newspaper.

Publication of school inspection reports proved to be a watershed in relationships between inspector and inspected. Prior to 1983, there was a professional, sometimes cosy, relationship and the worse that could happen from the school's point of view was that the local education authority advisers would pay more frequent visits to the school in order to discuss how to improve areas which had been subject to HMI criticism. After 1983, the stakes were much higher and the relationship between teachers and inspectors became more distant. Nevertheless, it was still statistically unlikely that an individual school would have a full inspection in any given year. In 1980, visits were made to 21 per cent of primary schools, 74 per cent of secondary schools and 45 per cent of special schools. Only 154 of these visits were full inspections. The comparable figures for 1990 were 17, 62 and 22 and only 92 of these visits resulted in inspection reports being published (Dunford, 1998, p. 100). Other demands on HMI were seriously eroding the time given to school inspection and the system was to suffer massive disruption as a result of the failure of HMI to give a sufficiently high priority to its core function.

It was a long-standing tenet of inspection that HMI reported as it found, but the publication of school inspection reports called into question the basis on which inspectors made their judgements. The Senior Chief Inspector, Sheila Browne, wrote:

> HMI's first duty is to record what is and to seek to understand why it is as it is. The second step is to answer the question whether or not it is good enough. To do so, HMI uses as a first set of measures the school's own aims

> and, as a second, those which derive from practice across the country and from public demand or aspiration. The two sets of measures are unlikely to be in general opposition but the circumstances of any individual institution or part of it may well lead to different emphases. (Browne, 1979)

In the words of a contemporary Department of Education and Science booklet, HMI 'offer the best professional judgements they can about what they see' (DES, 1983b, p. 3).

The assumption was that inspectors, as experienced educationists, recognised good and bad teaching, but this approach offered no guarantee of consistency, although inspectors achieved a degree of collegiality through their regular conferences and committees. Throughout the 1980s, there was no consensus about what constituted good teaching and there was no 'right' way of achieving success in a school. Indeed, it has been one of the strengths of the British education system, much admired in many other countries, that the school has had a high degree of autonomy in its aims and the manner in which it has set out to achieve them. The lack of consistency in HMI judgements was particularly evident in the reports on schools in disadvantaged areas. The head of one such school wrote: 'there seemed to be an assumption that, though methods must, of course, be adapted to suit the abilities of particular classes, the basic recipe should remain unchanged' (Barnes, 1983). Gray and Hannon's research on the first school inspection reports to be published in 1983 revealed that examination results were judged more harshly in schools with a disadvantaged intake. Comparisons with national and local averages, and overall pass rates, flattered the results in more advantaged schools. The examination performance of schools was rarely contextualised and pupil intake ability was glossed over in the judgements made by inspectors (Gray and Hannon, 1986). I replicated this research on reports published in 1989–90 and found that the quality of HMI judgements had not improved (Dunford, 1998, p. 105). There was clearly no guidance to reporting inspectors on how to present these statistics and it was not until 1991 that the format of school inspection reports was wholly standardised and examination results were presented in the same way. Even then, the results were not adequately contextualised.

With the increasing accountability of schools which took place during the 1980s, the publication of school inspection reports added greatly to the pressure on schools and this happened disproportionately for schools which served disadvantaged areas. One must draw the conclusion that HMI reporting methods added to the inequality under which such schools laboured.

LOCAL EDUCATION AUTHORITY INSPECTORS

During the 1980s there was no standard pattern of inspection and advisory services of LEAs. Time spent on lesson observation by LEA inspectors, for example, varied from 3 to 60 per cent. Most visits to schools by LEA inspectors did not result in a written report and full LEA inspections, unlike those by HMI after 1983, led to a report which was not published, even to the parents of the pupils in the school.

In 1979 there were 1,926 local authority advisers, but this number grew to 2,504 in 1988, by which time they were usually called inspectors. The pressure on LEAs to inspect their schools came from the Government, which was both increasing the accountability of schools and attempting to change radically the role of the LEA. Such inspections added to the pressure on schools and were rarely welcomed, especially in secondary schools. In primary education, LEA inspectors were generally successful former primary school headteachers whose judgements and opinions carried some weight with the teachers in the schools visited. In secondary education, the inspectors were generally former heads of department, who had moved into LEA posts as an alternative avenue of promotion. As the role of LEAs diminished during the 1980s, the quality of people taking inspection and advisory posts fell and those who had been longer in the advisory service often struggled for credibility with the teachers as curriculum and organisational changes in schools accelerated and some inspectors appeared to lose touch with current developments. This credibility gap was particularly apparent after the introduction of the National Curriculum in 1988. For heads of secondary schools, local authority inspection offered little, as there was the added problem that virtually no inspectors had previous experience of senior management in a school.

Where LEA inspectors could be useful was in the provision of advice on topics which were within their field of expertise. Before budgets were delegated to schools in 1990–91, this created an unacceptably patchy situation and many schools later welcomed the added flexibility which enabled them to buy in expertise from elsewhere in areas where the LEA service was considered to be lacking.

THE ADVISORY ROLE OF HMI

In the 1970s it was still possible to invite an HMI inspector into a school for a day in order to give advice. Between 1977 and 1983, the change from a regionally based structure of HMI to a national organisation gave individual inspectors much less flexibility in their work programmes. Offering advice remained one of their main functions, but this tended to be more in a national context and schools seeking advice were left to the vagaries of their local provision. The HMI Short Course programme for teachers remained in existence until the mid-1980s, but this function was gradually reduced and then removed, being overtaken by the devolution of training grants to schools and the provision of in-service training by a wide range of organisations. HMI was no longer seen as a readily available source of advice to individual schools. The Inspectorate did, however, greatly increase its published output during this period, and many useful booklets were produced, providing schools with both the rationale for and examples of good practice.

UNPLEASANT MESSAGES

When the National Curriculum was introduced in 1988, there was considerable doubt as to who would ensure that schools were delivering it. The LEAs, constantly under threat from the Government during this period, saw for themselves a potential role and this was somewhat surprisingly confirmed by the Government, which offered to provide finance, through Education Support Grants, for 300 extra LEA inspectors, who were to monitor individual schools, while HMI would continue to monitor educational provision on a national basis. The local authorities never received the money for the extra inspectors because the situation very soon changed.

Prior to 1988, the school curriculum was clearly the responsibility of the headteacher and inspection reports were an important part of the structure of accountability of heads and their staff. Following the introduction of the National Curriculum, some of that responsibility – particularly in relation to resources – fell on the Government itself. The huge increase in the centralisation of education policy which had occurred during the 1980s had its consequences for the Government in greater accountability. It was through the reports of HMI, and especially through the 1989 and 1990 annual reports of the Senior Chief Inspector, that this accountability reached its zenith. The Shadow Education Minister, Jack Straw, called the 1989 report 'an extraordinary and courageous indictment by Her Majesty's Inspectorate of Kenneth Baker's stewardship of the education service' (Dunford, 1998, p. 63). The report was particularly critical of the state of school buildings and drew attention to acute teacher shortages. In a thinly veiled reference to the criticism of teachers by Government Ministers, Eric Bolton wrote:

> Of great importance to most teachers, is that the work they do is seen to be valued and rated highly by society; that its difficulties are understood; and that teachers and education are not used as convenient scapegoats for all society's problems. Currently, too many teachers feel that their profession and its work are misjudged and seriously undervalued. (DES, 1989)

From the school's viewpoint, this represented welcome support and the comments on resources turned the spotlight of criticism on the Government. This seemed to teachers as the inevitable consequence of an under-resourced centralised system and HMI was seen as the champion of all those who had been pleading the case that schools were under-funded throughout the 1980s.

SHOOT THE MESSENGER

When Eric Bolton retired in 1991 as Senior Chief Inspector the process of appointing his successor was suspended by the then Secretary of State, Kenneth Clarke, in order to carry out a review of the role of HMI. At about the same time, the Prime Minister, John Major, produced the *Citizen's Charter*, which stated:

> If an Inspectorate is too close to the profession it is supervising there is a risk that it will lose touch with the interests of people who use the service. It may be captured by fashionable theories and lose the independence and objectivity that the public needs.
>
> Professional inspectorates can easily become part of a closed professional world. (Major, 1991)

Her Majesty's Inspectorate was clearly the target of this rhetoric, which divided the world into 'producers' and 'consumers' and placed the inspectorate firmly on the producer side. Those of us who were producers (although rejecting this pejorative terminology) did not see it like this at all, believing that HMI provided independent advice on the performance of schools, LEAs and Government. It was surely because the Government did not like the message which HMI published about the consequences of its increasingly centralist policies that it decided to shoot the messenger.

OFSTED: A NEW AGENDA

The Government was determined to champion the rights of the consumer and, with Ofgas to regulate the privatised gas industry, Ofwat for the water industry and Oftel for telecommunications, why not Ofsted for education? The Office for Standards in Education was created by the 1992 Education Act in order to increase the quantity of school inspection and thus add both to the accountability of schools and to the information available to parents on the performance of individual schools.

Instead of the haphazard and irregular programme of full inspections by HMI, schools were to be subjected to a four-year cycle of inspections, carried out by teams which would bid for the work. Money was taken away from LEAs in order to finance Ofsted and LEAs were thus forced to bid for Ofsted inspection work in order to finance their inspectorate and advisory services, although the latter faltered badly in most local authorities under the higher priorities of inspection and survival. Every Ofsted inspection team was to include a lay inspector, whose lack of professional experience of education was supposed to enable them to represent the consumer interest on each inspection team. The major role of HMI was to be the accreditation of inspection team leaders and it was also given the role of monitoring the work of the teams. This reduced role enabled the Secretary of State, Kenneth Clarke, to begin the slimming down of HMI from 480 to a target of 175 inspectors, although he made the transparently false claim that this reduction would strengthen HMI.

The first task of Ofsted was to produce a framework for the new-style inspections. This was written by HMI and was modelled closely on the *modus operandi* of a full HMI inspection. Its strength was that, for the first time, schools knew the criteria on which they were to be inspected. Furthermore, the *Framework* formed part of a comprehensive *Handbook for the Inspection of Schools*, which was a useful tool not only in preparing for inspection but also in evaluating existing structures and processes. Its main weakness, especially from the viewpoint of the primary school, was that it was really a model for inspecting secondary schools. Both inspectors and inspected found it almost impossible to adapt this ten-subject inspection model, without undue distortion, to the work of a small primary or special school. The four-year cycle for secondary schools started in September 1994 and in primary schools a year later, soon after which a National Inspection Advisory Group was formed by Ofsted to carry out a revision of the *Framework*. I served on this group, which commented on several drafts, but the second edition of the *Framework* which appeared in 1996 (Ofsted, 1995) bore little relation to the version which we had seen at the group's final meeting. Nevertheless, the new *Framework* was a great improvement on its predecessor.

Ofsted was conceived of by Kenneth Clarke as a vehicle for quality control in schools, and the management of Ofsted for the first 18 months tried to make some sense from a piece of legislation which had been rushed through Parliament, without much consultation, just before the 1992 general election. When, in 1994, Chris Woodhead moved from the School Curriculum and Assessment Authority to succeed Stewart Sutherland as Her Majesty's Chief Inspector for Schools in England, a change in atmosphere immediately occurred. Woodhead clearly had a strong agenda, not only for inspection as a device to raise standards in schools, but on pedagogy too. In his lectures, newspaper articles and official reports, he ruthlessly focused the attention of politicians and the general public, as well as teachers themselves, on the ways in which children were taught, especially in the primary school teaching of number and reading. He painted a bleak picture of standards in these basic skills.

Woodhead won the attention of newspaper editors, but lost the hearts of teachers, by claiming that 15,000 teachers were incompetent and should be sacked. In 1996 he changed the instructions to inspectors so that they were empowered to report to headteachers all lessons which were graded 1 and 2 (very good) and 6 and 7 (very poor). In 1997 this was extended and the grades of all lessons are reported to headteachers. The inspection of *teaching*, which had always been the rule under HMI, had become the inspection of *teachers* and another concern was added to the list of stress factors which teachers had to face.

With few exceptions, teachers are conscientious professionals. When an inspection is looming, they want to do well – for the children, for their colleagues and for the school – but teaching is an unpredictable business, where many things can go wrong, even in the best organised classroom. Few teachers are accustomed to being observed and graded (although lesson observation is becoming much more common in schools) and many perform nervously under such circumstances, especially if the inspector seems unsympathetic. Adding to the pressure, it has to be said, has been the attitude of some school governors and headteachers, who have felt the need to prepare for the inspection in a way which attempts to eliminate any chance of fault or criticism. Consultants and local authority inspectors have been called in to advise the staff on preparation – indeed, the market for inspection advice is more lucrative for Ofsted inspectors than the inspections themselves. In a letter to schools in 1998, David Blunkett, the current Secretary of State, stated that pre-Ofsted inspections were an unnecessary addition to teachers' workload and should be avoided. Striving for perfection is inherently stressful and the publicity given to inspection reports by local media makes the situation worse. When a school is working in difficult circumstances, it is very hard for teachers, and even more for the headteachers who must take the ultimate responsibility for success or failure, to avoid feelings of acute stress. The *Framework* specifies certain levels of pupil attendance and examination pass rates below which a school must be considered as having serious weaknesses. For schools in deprived areas, where the attainment of such performance thresholds is often very difficult, the potential for failure and its associated adverse publicity, both locally and nationally, goes well beyond the normal limits of professional accountability and quality control. This is made worse with the threat of return visits by HMI who monitor the progress of schools which are below the specified levels of performance and who can declare a school to be failing, even though it has previously had a satisfactory report from a routine Ofsted inspection. The 'naming and shaming' by the then Minister of State, Stephen Byers, in 1997 of 18 schools which had not shown sufficient improvement provided added pressure without making a positive contribution to the progress of the schools and no similar exercise was carried out in 1998.

Supporters of the Ofsted system of inspection argue that it offers schools an agenda for improvement and that it does not stifle initiative or impose uniformity. They claim that the system contains sufficient internal checks on the validity and reliability of individual judgements to overcome the disadvantage of having so many independent inspectors and teams. They also point to the wealth of information contained in the Ofsted database and the potential of this as an aid to school improvement and the spreading of good practice (Davis, 1996, p. 5).

Critics of the *Framework* believe that it is open to misinterpretation, that some features, such as spiritual development, are impossible to inspect objectively and thoroughly and that 'the *Framework* reduces a very complex and tentative business to ringing assertions of certainty' (Bowring-Carr, 1996, p. 42). Bowring-Carr believes that there is no prospect that Ofsted inspectors will be welded into the sort of interpretative community created through the collegiality of HMI although, as we have seen above, there was some inconsistency of judgement even within HMI (Bowring-Carr, 1996, p. 51). It has also been criticised on the grounds that it is costly, bureaucratic and authoritarian (SHA, 1996). In response to questionnaires issued by researchers and by Ofsted's own quality assurance department, most headteachers were positive about the contribution of the Ofsted process to the development of their school (Ouston *et al.*, 1996, p. 119). Other research suggests that classroom teachers were much less positive and notes the tendency for many schools to fall into a state of post-inspection exhaustion in which little real development takes place (Brimblecombe *et al.*, 1995, p. 133).

The 1992 Education Act established a parallel system of inspection in Wales, with the Office of Her Majesty's Chief Inspector (OHMCI) at the centre. The Chief Inspector in Wales from 1992 to 1997 was the widely respected Roy James, who had previously been the senior Welsh inspector. He has been succeeded by Susan Lewis, who was also a senior inspector. Comparisons of the annual reports of the Chief Inspectors in England and Wales suggest that there is a much more positive tone in Wales, whereas Chris Woodhead's reports tend to stress the negative.

Scotland was not included in the 1992 legislation and the role of HMI in Scotland remains much the same as in the 1980s. In fact, HMI in Scotland has always had a different role, being more closely involved with curriculum and other educational developments. The model of school inspection in Scotland is a balance of external inspection and school self-review, informed by statistical analysis of the school's performance by the HMI Audit Unit.

In the Channel Islands, both Jersey and Guernsey have an inspection model which is strongly rooted in school self-review.

THE FUTURE OF SCHOOL INSPECTION

Critics of the Ofsted system have suggested a number of improvements to the school inspection system. They believe that national and local inspection should be co-ordinated and that inspection and support should be clearly linked; that quality assurance in schools should be a combination of external inspection and school self-evaluation; that schools which are achieving specified targets should be inspected less frequently and that these targets should take into account previous performance and the context in which the school works (Dunford, 1998, p. 231).

While the Conservative Government was in office, the Labour Party put forward a range of proposals for the organisation of school inspection, including the establishment of an independent Education Standards Commission. By the time of the 1997 general election, the role of Ofsted had been so widely discussed and was so strongly supported in the press that it was seen as a bastion of support for the crusade to raise standards in schools. No one was more closely associated with this agenda than HMCI Chris Woodhead. It was therefore regrettable, but perhaps inevitable, that Ofsted survived in the same form and that Woodhead remained as HMCI, not only in the aftermath of the 1997 general election, but into a new four-year contract. The opportunity for a major review of school inspection, with wider discussion of the proposals put forward by Ofsted's critics, was lost and the 1998 Education Acts contained few measures of inspection reform, except for those which extended the role of Ofsted in the inspection of local education authorities and teacher training establishments. In Woodhead's letter of reappointment (18 September 1998), David Blunkett signalled a more flexible inspection regime for successful schools and gave explicit support to Woodhead's work in improving the quality and consistency of inspection judgements, implying that Ofsted's measures of quality control over its inspection teams were inadequate. Blunkett's letter also emphasised the importance of Ofsted's work in the areas of teacher training and local authority inspection.

School improvement occurs mainly through the actions of those who work in the schools themselves and, if inspection is to make the maximum contribution to school improvement, it must be integrated with processes of school self-review and evaluation. Neither the pre-1992 HMI system nor the more recent Ofsted structure attempted to introduce such an integrated system. The Labour Government may have had higher priorities for its first Education Acts than the reform of Ofsted, but it must be tackled in the longer term.

11

THE RISE OF PARENT POWER

ROBERT GODBER

The sovereignty of the consumer was a central tenet of Thatcherism; after 1979 client power became the driving force for change, not only in the private sector but also in the public services. Nowhere was this more evident than in education, nor was it anywhere more remarkable; the post-war settlement which followed the Butler Act gave overwhelming control to teachers and local education authorities, and the consumer interest was decidedly muted. Parents were accorded a passive role and were kept away from the 'secret garden' not only of the curriculum, but also of admissions and school governance. In the 1980s, all this was to change.

The catalyst was the perceived failure of comprehensive schools and the decline of confidence in the education system among employers and parents, as signalled by James Callaghan in his Ruskin College speech of 1976. It was Margaret Thatcher's Government, however, that set about making schools more accountable and yet more autonomous; one of her chosen instruments was the empowerment of parents both as customers exercising choice and as partners sharing the control of their children's schools. The parental dimension was a preoccupation of Conservative schools' policy through the Major years which followed and is part of the legacy left to Labour's education policy makers.

Parents' rights and expectations have been built on a huge platform of statutory provisions, from those governing admissions to those which specify what information must be contained in a prospectus. Some legislation, like the 1980 Act, which gave parents the formal right to express a preference of school, has had a revolutionary impact on the admissions policies of local education authorities; some has gradually added to the bank of information at parents' disposal. Some forms of civic redress had been available to parents long before the new order came in: schools' duty of care has been the subject of cases ever since parents sent their children to school. What is really significant is the cumulative effect of legislation upon public attitudes to the work of schools: the climate in which they operate has changed fundamentally. Parents, in particular, have become steadily more aware of their rights and their potential influence; for their part, schools have a heightened sensitivity to how their activities, policies and procedures are seen by parents.

CHOICE OF SCHOOL: PARENTAL PREFERENCE

The 1944 Education Act stated that pupils were to be 'educated in accordance with the wishes of their parents so far as is compatible with the provision of efficient instruction'. Its intention, however, became obscured by selection systems in some areas and the dirigiste policies of LEAs in others. Adherence to catchment areas, and the related planned admission limits (PALs), lay behind the varied performance of comprehensive schools in the 1960s and the right-wing 'Black Papers' (cf. Chapter 1 above) painted a dismal picture of pupils trapped in under-achieving comprehensive schools allegedly made worse by 'progressive' curricula and teaching methods. Making a reality of parental preference inspired much of Conservative education policy after 1979.

The 1980 Education Act established a formal right for parents to express a preference of school, supported by a right of appeal when preferences were not met. The implications of this legislation have been considerable for schools, LEAs and for parents themselves. The intention was explicit enough: to create a competitive market in which parents would be encouraged to 'shop around' for their children's schools, choosing according to their own criteria. Schools would respond by shaping and presenting their policies on curriculum organisation, behaviour and teaching styles so as to attract 'customers'; schools successful in attracting pupils would be full and those which failed to do so would have spare capacity and become vulnerable to closure. Subsequent legislation supported this approach, not least in equipping parents with the information and processes needed to exercise their rights.

The policy of parental preference was always presented as 'choice', but this was often a cruel charade as LEAs directed pupils across boroughs to schools which had empty places, while the school round the corner from their homes was oversubscribed. Local education authorities adopted different strategies for allocating places and some were slow to guarantee the right formally to express a preference at all. This was starkly illustrated by the *Rotherham Judgment* in the High Court in November 1997. A group of parents brought an action to resist the local authority's decision to allocate to their children places in a school which was not the one closest to their homes. It was held that the LEA acted unlawfully in not offering all parents in the borough an opportunity to express formally a preference of school. This caused the LEA to rerun its admissions procedure for the current year and to amend it radically for the future. The case demonstrates the readiness of parents to challenge decisions which they find inequitable, by litigation if need be, and even by reference to the ombudsman. Many more use the appeals procedure to overturn an allocation which they dispute, causing difficulties for schools when independent panels disregard clear advice that a given cohort is already above the standard number. One consequence of heightened parental awareness has been an increase in attempts by parents to move their children to different schools during the school year, again with management implication for schools.

Parents also make judgements about the respective merits of contiguous LEAs and some of their schools. This has resulted in a traffic of pupils across LEA boundaries and the publication of an unofficial league table of the importers and exporters of pupils. (The preoccupation with comparative tables led to some interesting variations on a theme: in one city, a local newspaper began publishing figures which showed the extent of over-subscription or surplus places in each school.) This raises interesting questions about the criteria used by parents in judging the comparative worth of schools. Performance information is often subsumed in the minds of parents as the more nebulous 'good reputation', which may also include the existence of school uniform, whether or not a school has a sixth form, or the effectiveness of its pastoral system. The criteria may vary according to social class, with middle-class parents valuing academic factors above, say, proximity to home.

Basing so much on parental preference has had a major impact on school organisation in some areas, notably at secondary level. The appeal of grant-maintained status was closely related to a school's wish to free itself in order to adjust to the demands of consumer parents, not least in reviving the previously dormant issue of selection. The wild vision of 'a grammar school in every town', which afflicted John Major, was at once a mistaken assumption that parents would welcome it, and at the same time a cavalier disregard for the wider planning of school provision. Even where there were no grant-maintained schools, the embedded culture of parental choice gave LEAs many strategic problems. Bids which sought to provide more places at a popular school were dismissed by the DfEE because the neighbouring school had spare capacity. Thus Labour has inherited a serious mismatch between public policy and public administration which raised parental demand and then failed to meet it.

The importance of parental preference in the public mind has been underlined in the media by the schooling decisions of some public figures, notably those in politics. Tony Blair's choice of a Catholic boys' school in a different part of London, Harriet Harman's preference for a selective school in another borough and William Hague's as yet partly hypothetical assertion that a decent local comprehensive can do the job perfectly well, and at lower cost than an independent school, all focus on aspects of the debate, and do so in the spotlight of media interest. They may not ease the making of public policy, but they act as loud promptings to parents considering the exercise of their recently acquired rights.

GOVERNANCE: THE INVOLVEMENT OF PARENTS

Entirely consistent with Conservative ideas about parents as 'stakeholders' in schools was the place created for them in school governance. The revolution in the composition of governing bodies, coupled with the impact of local management, has transformed the way schools are governed and the key factor has been the election of parent governors. The old 'municipal' model for schools was a wholly dominant bench of LEA political nominees, many of them majority group councillors, augmented by a few token governors from 'community' interests such as the churches and universities. Their relative powerlessness meant that these dispositions provoked little hostile comment, but they would have proved inadequate as vehicles for devolved governance. The 1980 Act reflected the Government's concern to empower parents as the most likely enforcers of Conservative legislation. From then, representation on governing bodies mirrored the principal interests involved, and in carefully balanced proportions. In a typical LEA-maintained secondary school, the LEA nominates five governors, parents elect five and teachers two. A further six are co-opted. In a grant-maintained school the position is similar, but with provision for foundation governors. During the 1980s, then, parents enjoyed a distinctive voice in the governance of their children's schools but, after a period of initial enthusiasm, this voice has varied in volume and stridency.

These arrangements have given parents an unprecedented opportunity;

although the allocation of seats seems to prevent any particular group dominating the governing body, the reality in many cases is that the parent perception prevails. Where the LEA nominations are delegated to the local ward parties, those asked to serve include parents or former parents and, where the ethos of the governing body is strong, parent governors whose term of office has ended will often seek to be co-opted. This writer's current governing body consists of 19 members, of whom 14 are parents or past parents. This is not, of course, necessarily typical; in some LEAs political nominations will ensure a higher profile for debates within the LEA itself, the number of councillors on governing bodies may be significantly higher and the school may have difficulty in attracting sufficient parents to fill vacancies. Longevity of service by those who begin as parent governors will depend upon the quality of chair and of governor training. Quality of experience as a governor inevitably affects length of service, but the parent lobby is usually the strongest.

THE CHANGED ROLE OF GOVERNING BODIES

The 1986 Education Act fundamentally altered the role of governing bodies in maintained schools. It allocated specific functions and defined the relationship between head, governors and LEA. Thus it set up the model of governance which, subject to changes made in the 1996 Act, remains in place. It was central to the Conservatives' drive to divest LEAs of some of their powers by devolving them upon governors who, it was assumed, would have a sure feel for the ethos and philosophy of their school. Governing bodies were to be the vehicles for local management of schools (LMS), exercising key powers delegated by the LEA, notably on staffing and finance.

A critical but difficult distinction has been crucial to the success or failure of this model of governance: that between policy and day-to-day management of the school. Governors are responsible for the evolution and monitoring of policy and headteachers are responsible for management within the framework laid down by the policy of the governing body. In practice, this is not a clear distinction. Wise governing bodies have relied heavily on the professional advice of LEAs and heads and good relationships have been central to the success of these arrangements. Effective monitoring of policy implementation has proved to be the basis for effective governance, but this has depended on the level of mutual trust between the head and the chair of governors.

Effective ways of working with governors have developed in schools under local management. Other senior teachers have attended governing body meetings and sub-committees and governors have been involved in the life of the school, so that they are well informed and have a profile among staff and pupils commensurate with their constitutional role. Opportunities to work with teachers, say on uniform policy or a post-Ofsted action plan, can be found, so that a policy, once published as belonging to the governors (as properly it does), has a sense of ownership among the staff. Governors need support from senior managers in the school and from an effective local governors' organisation. These are affiliated to one of the national governors' organisations, enabling governors to lobby on behalf of the interest they serve.

Setting the school budget is a central function of governing bodies and, against a background of severe funding constraints, they have had to take responsibility for some hard choices: staffing, curriculum provision, maintenance and repair have all competed for precious resources. Constrained by employment law and the statutory obligations of the National Curriculum, governors have found themselves with onerous decisions. This scale of responsibility has placed strain on local management of schools and has caused anxiety about governor recruitment.

Whatever the difficulties, however, the pivotal role of governors is likely to remain. Governors' organisations are keen to defend the importance of the role of governing bodies and headteachers have no desire to see the reinvention of paternalistic and intrusive LEAs. The Labour Government's legislative plans do little to disturb the present system. Indeed, the responsibilities of governing bodies grow with their agendas. Most recently, it has become the duty of the governing body to set targets for its school and to forge a new relationship with the LEA in pursuit of higher standards of school performance. New Labour has been very willing to pick up the baton handed to it by the previous Government.

ACCOUNTABILITY: ANSWERING TO PARENTS

Wise headteachers have always developed well-trained antennae with which to sense parental concerns, actual or potential; even before 1979, some heads involved parents actively in the life of the school. Practice among LEAs varied considerably, with some relying entirely on the local electoral process to inform them hazily of what parents as members of the electorate believed. The strong perception in the Conservative Party in the 1970s was that parents were either ignored, defied or subjected to occasional and wholly spurious consultations. How they were treated depended too much on where they happened to live and which school their children attended. After 1979, Conservative Governments erected a substantial platform of parents' statutory rights which has placed equally weighty, even onerous, responsibilities on heads and governors to account to parents for their stewardship. These responsibilities are clearly stated, have grown over the years and are evident in many crucial aspects of school life. They are based on the unquenchable assumption that parents can use a vast amount of information and on the incontestable belief that in a democratic society the right to information has very broad limits. The requirement in the 1989 regulations for heads to make available a large amount of specified information is the bedrock of this philosophy.

Central to this model of accountability, however, was the governors' annual report to parents and the annual parents' meeting. The Education (No. 2) Act 1986 required the governing body of every LEA-maintained school to report to parents on the discharge of its functions and to hold an annual meeting to discuss the contents of this report. Similar provisions apply to grant-maintained schools. The content of the annual report is largely prescribed and the degree of prescription has increased; the DfEE Circulars 11/96 and 12/96 added three more specific requirements to the 19 which already existed, including the extent to which the school had achieved its sporting aims over the previous year. It is hard to avoid the sense that the symbolic, almost ritualistic, value of the compilation of the report eclipses any practical use it might have. As a document of record, it requires the governors to demonstrate publicly that they have carried out their duties with probity and appropriate care on each of several counts, but its readership may be small and disengaged. The annual parents' meeting is a similar rite of passage through the school year, at which governors often outnumber parents and attendances are insufficient to carry resolutions. Its friends can claim that it acts as a safety valve – a device which can signal concerns – and is therefore of considerable constitutional value. For those few and inveterate questioners on such occasions, it makes for face-to-face accountability and, despite the consensus among teachers' associations that otherwise it serves little purpose, it has enjoyed the protection of being politically untouchable.

The Parents' Charter, which first appeared in 1991, spelt out the Government's intention to make information about schools more accessible, thus providing hard evidence on which parents could base their decisions on school preferences. Subsequent regulations have governed the publication of comparative performance tables for public examinations, absences and the results of National Curriculum assessments. The annual publication of this information has added a new seasonal date to the national calendar, alongside the Budget, the Trooping of the Colour and the Grand National. For all their acknowledged crudity, the five A–C GCSE scores – league tables being based on the percentage of 15 year olds in each school achieving 5 GCSE passes at grades A–C – have become the key benchmark, and the principal users of the information are parents – precisely as intended. Statutory provisions were introduced to govern how and when schools should report to parents on their children's progress; here again, the intention was to empower parents who considered that information from schools was inadequate or lacking in clarity. Behind such provision was the political suspicion that 'recording of achievement' had become a means of obfuscation rather than lucidity.

On school prospectuses, the 1994 regulations followed a similar theme. Croner's *Head's Legal Guide* lists no fewer than 19 categories of information which a prospectus needs to provide. Schools had already recognised the marketing potential of their prospectuses and had invested both money and ingenuity in their production; many a local printer must be grateful to the marketplace in school choice which successive Conservative Education Secretaries of State had reinforced. For many schools the attractively presented, artistically designed colour brochure, which would once have been the province of the tour operator, has become one component of a presentational strategy, in which a house style in publications has been cultivated. The audience, of course, is the parent, present and future (past, too, it should be said, because satisfied customers recommend schools to their friends). Perhaps nothing better symbolises the acknowledgment of 'parent power' than the attention now given to a school's prospectus, which seems a world away from the minimal, monochrome and almost sheepish document which it has superseded.

In view of the many other statutory rights given to parents, it is hardly surprising that they were given a part in the new model of school inspection in the Education Act 1992. Important elements in an Ofsted inspection are the questionnaire to parents and the parents' meeting with the registered inspector. To compare attendance at this meeting with that at the annual parents' meeting is to see how fully parents recognise their potential for influencing the report and very probably the school's response to it. Significantly, the amendments to the Ofsted inspection pattern, effective from September 1997, have sought to increase parental input during the inspection week itself. Teachers' scepticism of inspection reports is not altogether shared by parents and, more significantly perhaps, by potential parents of a school. These documents are scanned with interest by those 'looking at several possibilities', and when I recently offered an inquirer a copy of the summary of a very recent inspection report, she politely asked for the full version. It is not unusual for heads of schools to be cross-examined by a parent who has taken as a reference the last inspection report on the school.

If access to information is indeed power, then parents were hugely empowered by 18 years of Conservative Government. Inevitably, those parents who benefited most were middle class, those with expectation and ambition, and with the capacity to collate and use the information available. But the real significance of the opening up of the 'secret garden' is that it has produced a cultural revolution which has touched a very wide audience. Not only has it genuinely enfranchised more parents in their dealings with schools, it has given them greater articulacy. The response of schools has been what the Conservative Governments of Margaret Thatcher and John Major most wanted: to embed an awareness of parental interest deep into the management thinking of the school. Parents' reactions are now as central to school policy making as once they were peripheral, and there are some obvious effects: uniforms have staged a comeback, albeit as 'dress codes' in many cases; schools take pains to explain their actions and policies more carefully; discipline codes rely heavily on parental support; policies on homework allocate a role to parents. In the main, complaints are handled with sensitivity and skill, rather than being dismissed as trouble-making. The overwhelming majority of parents are broadly supportive and understanding (perhaps some Conservatives are struck by the irony that their revolution has built a greater empathy for teachers and schools). The fear of overdemanding and importunate parents is the cross which schools must bear.

A DUTY OF CARE: LITIGIOUS PARENTS

Schools have found themselves more vulnerable to threats of litigation from parents. While this cannot be seen, presumably, as an intention of public policy, there is nonetheless a discernible link between rising parental expectations of what schools should do for their children, and the sanctions which parents can deploy when schools appear to fall short of their civil law duty of care when acting *in loco parentis*. Parents have been encouraged to reconsider their relationship with their children's schools in respect of purely educational matters (the curriculum, reporting levels of attainment, and so on); it would have been naive to imagine that this would have had no effect on the level of the schools' responsibility for the physical welfare of children. While successive Conservative administrations were strengthening the role of parents over the management of education in schools, other social forces were making them aware of the wider responsibilities which schools have towards pupils as part of a community.

It is a truism that we have become a more litigious society and this is in part because we are a less deferential one. Citizens are less likely to put up with perceived injustice and are more aware of how best to seek redress. As the basis of the relationship between parents and schools becomes more closely defined in law, so resort to litigation, or threatened litigation, becomes steadily more probable. The management of exclusions well illustrates this point, not least because legal practices have increasingly found scope for their services in this field. Heads have experienced in the last two decades the extension of health and safety legislation, just as some aspects of school provision have become hugely sensitive to legal resort. The management of school journeys is typical of this. The solicitor's letter on behalf of a parent is no longer the collector's item it once was. Schools have rightly become much more alert to the possible interpretations of their duty of care and the work of the health and safety officer has assumed major importance. Two factors have recently contributed to raising awareness among parents and schools. One, ironically, is that years of neglect of school premises have piled up all kinds of hazards at a time when parents are becoming more conscious of their rights as consumers, so that leaking roofs are no longer an irritant but a threat to safety. Parental tolerance of malodorous toilets and broken fitments is very properly declining and some schools have been happy to enlist the support of parents in pushing for improvements in working conditions. A second factor is the unfortunate necessity to focus on school security, following recent tragedies and the steady rise in cases of intrusion on to school premises. Parents have a right to expect that their children should be reasonably safe at school and are increasingly prepared to question what LEAs and schools are doing to ensure this.

Neither LEAs nor schools welcome adverse publicity and are aware that a news-hungry local newspaper or radio station may be receptive to an approach from an aggrieved parent. More often than not, an angry threat will not be carried out and a cautious editor will wisely steer clear of involvement in a vendetta, but there is always the risk that a newsy story will strike a chord with the public and damage the school. Recourse to the media may be linked to possible litigation and then the story may have more potential. Most parents in dispute with their child's school are not motivated by any desire for publicity; the vast majority seek fair redress and will be content with due process and the usual levels of discretion. However, where a case reaches the courts and teachers are called as witnesses to face counsel, the outcome can be traumatic.

Faced with, and usually agreeing with, parental concerns about care issues, LEAs and schools can will the ends but not always the means. Dangerous premises require funding if their hazardous condition is to be appropriately repaired. However, where the need is to have policies and procedures in place, the response has been prompt and genuine. Behaviour management initiatives have generally anticipated parental concern rather than followed it. Assiduity in following such procedures has been built into the culture of schools, especially where headteachers have insisted upon it. Accident reporting, for instance, has been done more carefully and teachers are aware that an accusation of inadequate supervision can trigger parental action which is well-informed and appropriately advised. A court case concerning responsibility for pupils left by parents at the school gate well before the start of the school day neatly illustrates the blurred boundary between parental and school duty of care. Most schools benefit from the goodwill which allows the concerns of parents and the caring professionalism of teachers to work effectively together for the benefit of pupils.

THE CONSERVATIVE LEGACY AND LABOUR'S INHERITANCE: MORE POWERFUL PARENTS

Croner's *Head's Legal Guide* makes this balanced judgement about the relationship between parents and teachers:

> Parents must trust teachers and the duty of teachers to earn that trust is moral rather than legal. Teachers should therefore be reasonably tolerant of parental representation . . . it is now commonly accepted that parents have a major part to play in education and there is statutory provision for their involvement.

The empowerment of parents ran through the Conservative years after 1979 as a consistent theme. The Tories expected much from their programme of enfranchisement and were perhaps rather disappointed with the somewhat muted response of parents, many of whom did not take advantage of their newly acquired rights as much as successive Secretaries of State might have wished. Parents have not behaved as the stick to beat the educational establishment that some Tories expected; indeed, there emerged a stronger partnership between parents and schools, based on a sounder understanding of the difficulties of schools. Parents have, generally, surveyed the apparatus before them and have used it selectively; they have taken a major part in school government but have declined to examine every last dot and comma of school management. They have taken those pieces of information which they have found useful, like the broad thrust of performance tables and the outcomes of inspections, but have shrewdly recognised the limitations of these. Overall, they have applied sensible judgements about their children's schools. Are they happy? Are they making progress? Are they developing as people? As customers in the marketplace, parents have performed only moderately well, partly because it is a far from perfect market. Oversubscription of some popular schools and spare places in the less favoured have produced problems of planning and investment for LEAs. Notably, parents have not led the charge towards grant-maintained status, as they were expected to do; on the contrary, they have in many cases conspicuously dragged their feet.

The Labour Government sees parents as natural allies in its drive for improved performance by schools and there is no evidence that Ministers intend to dismantle any of the significant powers held by parents. Indeed, where notable changes are envisaged, parents are to be key players; the balloting of parents with children in feeder primary schools on the future of grammar schools is ample testimony to that. The right of parents to express preference for schools is politically sacrosanct, although the Government will need to address the problems presented by undersubscribed schools; so too with school governance, parental representation is seen as essential and a National Parents' Council may eventually give parents influence on policy making at national level, where the National Confederation of Parent Teacher Associations has conspicuously failed to make its mark, largely owing to allegations of financial irregularities and internal strife within the NCPTA itself. The battery of information available to parents is likely to be refined, not replaced. Thus far, David Blunkett has been more inclined to offend teachers than to upset parents.

Parents and their perceptions are now much closer to the business of school government than ever before and it is unlikely that this will be reduced. Equally, however, it is unlikely that they will be drawn nearer the centre. Generally, parents recognise that schools know their business and should be reasonably free to discharge it, subject to the safeguards now in place. It is seen as prudent that those parents who wish to do so should interest themselves in school governance and that all should be able to take a healthy interest in their child's school, to which they are naturally drawn. Most parents, once they have exercised any preference they may have, will want to have some kind of redress if things threaten to go wrong. Beyond that, the maxim that 'silence gives consent' will usually prevail. For parents, we now have an inclusive settlement, which is in sharp contrast with the 1944 legislation which enabled them to be excluded by those schools which wished to do so.

12

CHALLENGING PARTNERS: CENTRAL GOVERNMENT, LOCAL GOVERNMENT AND SCHOOLS

HEATHER DU QUESNAY

From the mid-1980s, for almost ten years, successive Conservative Governments delighted in portraying themselves as the implacable opponents of local education authorities (LEAs). With the support of most of the media, they laid at the door of LEAs the faults of the public education service, as they perceived them, while simultaneously stripping local government of both its powers and its self-confidence. In vain did local government call for some acknowledgement of the traditional central–local partnership in the administration of education. It seemed sometimes that LEAs were allowed to survive only because they were such useful scapegoats when things went wrong. Yet local government can thank the Conservatives for forcing it to get its educational act together. Without that sustained pressure it might not have been anywhere near as ready to meet the challenges of the Blair administration, and Blair is potentially no less demanding a judge than his predecessors.

Margaret Thatcher and her colleagues were at best impatient with the bureaucratic deadweight which they perceived to be at the heart of much local government. In London and some of the other great cities the feeling was one of more active loathing for the antics of so-called 'loony-left' councils, whose extreme political views pitched them into head-to-head conflict with central government, while the local services for which they were responsible descended into a shambles of incompetence, inefficiency and, in some cases, overt corruption. Even so, the early initiatives of the Thatcher Government to curtail the powers of local education authorities were pretty tentative, consisting principally of tidying up the role of school governing bodies and giving parents the right to express a preference for a school in the 1980 Education Act.

There were some omens around like the introduction in 1984 of specific grants to support LEA expenditure in areas targeted by central government (eventually designated Grants for Education Support and Training – GEST) which were rightly read by shrewd local politicians as the beginnings of central government encroachment on LEAs' freedom of manoeuvre. But the legislation which was really to transform roles and relationships within the public education system did not reach the statute book until a full nine years had passed after Margaret Thatcher became Prime Minister. The Education Reform Bill 1987 was nicknamed 'Gerbil' (the Great Education Reform Bill) by educationists as it made its way through the various stages of the parliamentary process, the derisive label reflecting the boldness of those who whistle in the dark to keep the shadows at bay.

The 1988 Act was characterised by a mixture of centralising (National Curriculum, pupil testing at 7, 11 and 14, restrictions on LEA admission policies) and devolutionary (local management of schools, grant-maintained status, city technology colleges) tendencies. There were those who saw its rationale as lying in nothing more sophisticated than a determination to squeeze local government out of the education system. However, local education authorities showed themselves to be remarkably adaptable. They came fairly rapidly to live with, indeed to welcome, much of the Act. One provision, though, aroused almost universal hostility, and that was the power created for schools to opt out of their local education authority's control into grant-maintained status. Even the choice of words caused offence, for few councillors and officers in local government liked to see their relationship with schools in terms of control or constraint.

The unexpected impact of the Education Reform Act has been widely noted, in as much as it led to a wave of opting out in areas which had traditionally been associated with Conservative political dominance (Essex, Kent, Bromley, for example), while many traditional Labour councils from which Mrs Thatcher's Government had hoped to 'liberate' schools had little difficulty in maintaining the status quo. What is less often acknowledged is the galvanising effect that the availability of grant-maintained status had on LEAs themselves. The pressure from headteachers for improved services and a right to be consulted; the increasing confidence and strength of governing bodies; and the transparency of information which schools demanded about budget matters transformed the way most LEAs did their business.

Responding to such pressures and developing new styles of working with headteachers and governors were enormously stimulating. With greater or lesser alacrity, LEAs developed a 'customer culture' whereby it was recognised that schools were properly in the driving seat when it came to the selection and purchasing of services designed to support them. The pressures on LEA staff were very considerable, particularly on those such as advisers and inspectors, who had traditionally operated from a power base of authority. Some proved incapable of adjusting to the new regime, while others thrived on the ambiguities of the requirement to deliver challenging judgements while retaining market share.

At the level of support services to schools, then, the Government's policies were almost entirely beneficial, but at a strategic level the Education Reform Act gravely inhibited the governance of the system. The power of LEAs to deal with difficult issues such as school reorganisation and the removal of surplus places was severely curtailed by the fact that schools could seek grant-maintained status as an alternative to closure. The resulting policy gridlock was graphically described by the Audit Commission in its report *Trading Places* (Audit Commission, 1997). Likewise, the proliferation of admissions authorities and admissions policies made secondary school entry a nightmare for parents in areas where grant-maintained status took off. More widely felt was the constraining effect of grant-maintained status on general LEA policy making: the possibility of schools opting out was, rightly or wrongly, perceived as a serious threat to the stability of the system by many LEAs and that made it extremely difficult for them to take any decision that might have been interpreted as hostile, or even tough, by schools. Once Kenneth Clarke and John Patten began more actively to encourage schools to consider grant-maintained status, there was a real risk of the constructive partnership which had begun to develop between schools and LEAs under local management becoming an unwitting provider-side conspiracy.

The revolution affecting LEAs was not limited to schools. Local education authorities had started to lose other powers and responsibilities from 1988 when the Education Reform Act led to the removal of higher education colleges and polytechnics from local government control. In subsequent years, further education colleges (1992) followed them and the careers service was put out to contract in 1993. Other players entered the scene nationally: the National Curriculum Council and the School Examinations and Assessment Council (to be succeeded by the School Curriculum and Assessment Authority) followed hard on the 1988 Act; the Funding Agency for Schools was established by the Act of 1993 to oversee the planning and funding of the grant-maintained sector and the

Teacher Training Agency appeared following legislation in 1994. The latter was primarily the result of a redistribution of powers at national level but it impinged directly on LEAs through its interest in in-service training, over which they had previously presided supreme, and in its introduction and regulation of qualifications for headteachers.

Of all the new national players, by far the most significant for both LEAs and schools was Ofsted, which Chris Woodhead was appointed to lead as Her Majesty's Chief Inspector of Schools (HMCI) in 1994. Even under Sir Stewart Sutherland, the first HMCI, LEAs were deeply uncomfortable about the new inspection arrangements, resenting, as they did, the weakening in the Schools Act 1992 of their own power to inspect and the accompanying loss of resources to the national agency. However, as Chris Woodhead took hold of Ofsted and honed his skills in providing the media with telling soundbites, relationships became increasingly strained. Woodhead portrayed LEAs as a drag on schools' progress, using the Socratic method of questioning to lead his audience to a negative conclusion. In a pamphlet written for the right-wing think-tank, Politeia, he states that 'the issue of local management and the grant maintained initiative calls into question the impact, role and indeed continuing existence of the local education authority' (Woodhead, 1995). He then quotes at length Brian Sherratt, the head of Great Barr Grant-Maintained School in Birmingham, whose comments include a scathing description of 'the dependency culture created by education authorities . . . Authorities dress up this dependency as a spurious kind of partnership – the family of schools. But the dependency culture reproduces dependent people, not partners; the authority is always there.'

Woodhead's view of the importance of schools taking responsibility for their own standards and development was more widely shared than he cared to acknowledge. But the extreme terms in which he advanced his views often prompted debates which were more acrimonious than illuminating. Woodhead's sceptical stance gave succour to the anti-local government prejudices of certain politicians and sections of the media. However, schools and LEAs found themselves bound together by a shared experience – that of being lashed by the Chief Inspector's tongue.

Meanwhile, throughout the Conservative years, local government funding was under continuous pressure, partly as a result of central government mistrust of the lower tier and partly as a consequence of the wider drive to reduce public spending. The removal of further education from local government control coincided with the abolition of the community charge which had been a substantial part of Margaret Thatcher's undoing and further education was seen by many in local government as a casualty of the drive to introduce council tax. Local government had already lost the power directly to levy a rate on local businesses and was now responsible for raising only about a quarter of its revenue from local taxation. Central government bore down hard even on this revenue-raising power through a tightly managed discipline of assessing the expenditure needs of councils and capping the amount by which councils could increase their local taxes.

It would hardly be surprising if, as a result of this onslaught, both press and public questioned the efficacy of local government's role in education. Nor is it surprising that the self-confidence of local politicians and officers was rocked by the frequent and debilitating criticism from on high. Yet other things were happening. The seeds of the LEAs' resurgence were sown by the very Act which had apparently signalled their demise. In the years following 1988, simply because it was extremely difficult for LEAs to do anything without the agreement of the schools, LEA officers and members became adept at developing consensual styles of working. Many LEAs attempted to describe the nature of their relationship with the schools in the form of partnership agreements which articulated the values they shared. Despite the disapproval of parts of the grant-maintained sector, in some areas GM schools chose to be associated with aspects of the new partnership agenda. Moreover, the challenge to convince schools that it was worth being part of an LEA was such that LEAs had to give priority to the continuous improvement of their service. Some began to experiment with a variety of arrangements for the delivery of support services, including the involvement of the private sector, pragmatically seeking out the best quality of service at the best price. These changes increased schools' confidence in what the LEA had to offer and a new shared dynamic developed for service improvement.

Almost imperceptibly at first, at least as far as the national debate was concerned, LEAs and schools began to develop new strategies for raising the standard of pupils' attainment. Thus it was that when the more pragmatic and conciliatory Gillian Shephard became Secretary of State in 1994, there was a wealth of strategies for the DfEE's new School Improvement Unit to draw on. They included the setting of numerical targets to raise attainment, the use of benchmarking to enable schools to compare themselves with others of a similar character and the involvement of governing bodies in scrutinising the performance of their school. Ironically, it was probably the outcome of Ofsted's work that did most to convince Mrs Shephard that a body outside the school was required to raise standards: how else was she to deal with the increasing number of failing schools put into special measures by the inspection system? So it came about that the Conservatives' final education White Paper included a chapter on the role of local education authorities (DfEE, 1996b). However, the sympathy of Mrs Shephard and some of her Ministers for the LEA's role continued to be submerged in the anti-local government rhetoric which emanated from most of the Government, including the Prime Minister himself. The introduction, apparently against Mrs Shephard's wishes, and against the almost unanimous advice of LEAs, of vouchers for nursery education, announced shortly before the final White Paper, showed just how embattled the Secretary of State was.

The legacy which Labour inherited in 1997, then, included the following features: a National Curriculum which was largely accepted as a basic statement of what children were entitled to learn and teachers required to teach; a system of pupil testing at 7, 11, and 14 which was bedding down, despite the continued protestations of a few of the more extreme teacher representatives, and which enabled a systematic national and local overview of pupil performance to be taken for the first time; a thriving system of local management which had proved its worth in enabling schools to develop a greater sense of responsibility for their own destiny and which had consolidated the role and power of governing bodies; an inspection system which was driving home the message of public accountability and undeniably revealing failures that had to be addressed, but which nonetheless was regarded with fear and distrust by many in the education system. As to the LEAs, while their statutory powers had been significantly attenuated, they had begun to discover new ways of working and to explore the impact of partnership, persuasion and influence, the very skills which the new Government would soon be calling for from local government.

The Labour Government was also heir to a system that was more divided and fragmented than at any time since the 1944 Act. Schools in many areas had become more accustomed to competing with each other than to sharing good practice. The fact that grant-maintained schools were responsible for setting their own admissions policies, as voluntary-aided (church) schools had always done, meant that a variety of admissions authorities existed in some parts of the country, defying ease of access to all but the most accomplished parents. Above all, the Conservative emphasis on the supremacy of the market and on funding systems driven primarily by pupil numbers, with minimal recognition of social need, left the system ill-equipped to mediate in areas of social disadvantage. Moreover, the education policies of successive Conservative Governments which were dominated by a preoccupation with schools, together with the pressure of budget constraints, had led some local education authorities, albeit reluctantly, to neglect their wider educational responsibilities, and to become to a greater or lesser extent school-centric, aggravating the historic difficulty which local councils had experienced in achieving cooperation and synergy between education and other local services. Likewise, at national level, despite the belated amalgamation in the Conservatives' final term, of the Departments of Education and Employment, the civil service continued to operate in the narrow policy chimneys which Sir Geoffrey Holland, when Permanent Secretary, had, in somewhat mandarin fashion, likened to the towers of San Gimignano in their failure to achieve horizontal connections. Even more than LEAs, the DfEE was struggling to find coherence within its own agenda, let alone with other Departments.

Labour's first education White Paper continued the school-centric agenda of the Tories. *Excellence in Schools* (DfEE, 1997a) was substantially composed by the Standards and Effectiveness Unit of the DfEE, a new creation of the Labour Government. Led by Professor Michael Barber, who was seconded into the Department with the formal status of a political adviser, it has been known to describe itself as the 'LEA for LEAs'. The description of the LEA's role bears some echoes of the previous Government's policy in its emphasis upon 'intervention in inverse proportion to success'. Indeed, Ministers' anxiety that local councils might seek a return to the bad old days of bureaucratic control and interference in the affairs of schools was almost palpable, aggravated no doubt by the grant-maintained lobby whose fear of regression, or indeed, retribution, following their return to the LEA system, was much in evidence. Concern was such that a 47-page draft *Code of Practice on LEA–School Relations* was published (DfEE, 1998), perhaps mainly to offer reassurance to the grant-maintained sector.

In fact, the principal roles outlined for the LEA in the 1997 White Paper reflect pretty well the way in which LEAs' business has developed in the past ten years. They are summarised as leading the drive to raise standards through the application of an appropriate balance of pressure and support to schools, together with a range of administrative functions such as organising education outside school; planning the supply of school places; setting overall school budgets; organising services to support individual pupils, such as transport and welfare services; and supplying services such as personnel and finance advice for schools to buy. A separate White Paper (DfEE, 1998) sets out the Government's expectations with regard to children with special educational needs.

The standards agenda depends increasingly on the use of objective measures of pupils' attainment, building on the introduction of regular testing by the previous Government. Analysis of performance, not only at LEA and school level, but also for classes and individual pupils, is now taken for granted. LEAs are expected to take a lead in analysing and interpreting this data and in helping schools to use it intelligently to make management judgements and set targets for improvement. The School Standards and Framework Act 1998 will require LEAs to publish the improvement targets set by each school, together with overall targets for the LEA as a whole, in an Education Development Plan for their area.

The Education Development Plan will be the first big test of the LEA–schools partnership under the new Government. There is a certain gap in the thinking which only the LEA can bridge: Ministers and the DfEE set the targets for the LEA (or, at least in the case of literacy, offer the LEA a range) but schools set their own targets. Local education authorities will have the task of persuading schools to set targets in line with the LEA aggregate. And the schools will have very different expectations: some, like Great Barr, may continue to be wary of old-style bureaucracy and the dependency culture, while others may see themselves primarily as customers for LEA services or regard the LEA as a source of uncritical support. But all will have to move forward fast if the national targets are to be attained. The cynic may say that the LEAs are being set up to fail. The enthusiasm of their early response does not suggest that they see it in that way. But the delicacy of their task needs to be recognised: it is time for partnership to come of age.

In its first year, Labour has been no softer on the inspection regime than the previous Government. Despite a lengthening of the school inspection cycle from four years to six, already agreed by the Conservatives, there is no evidence that the new Government is any less ready than the last to hold schools to public account. One of the first acts of the new Schools Minister, Stephen Byers, was to 'name and shame' 18 schools which had been put into special measures by Ofsted and about whose progress he was dissatisfied. Local education authorities too began to feel the bite of an inspection regime, which was instituted by the Conservatives in the Education Act 1997. The legislation followed early pilot inspections into which LEAs had entered voluntarily. Some of the pilots, like those in Staffordshire and Kirklees, were carried out within a framework developed by the Association of Chief Education Officers (ACEO, 1997), but inevitably those which hit the headlines were the inspections of LEAs where serious public concern had arisen about standards: Calderdale, initiated by Gillian Shephard, and Hackney, shortly after Labour came to power.

Under the terms of the Education Act 1997, Ofsted appears to be the senior partner in the inspection of LEAs, with the Audit Commission adopting a subordinate role. However, the publication by the Commission of a 'think-piece' on the role of local education authorities, *Changing Partners* (Audit Commission, 1998), may herald a renewal of its interest in the education activities of local government. The Commission's greater involvement in LEA inspection would be welcome for a number of reasons. First, the replacement of compulsory competitive tendering by a best value regime, under which local government will be required to match the performance of its services against national comparators, will put a new emphasis on economy, efficiency and value for money. These are qualities which the Audit Commission has long experience of measuring: the lack of an overt methodology for judgements about value for money in Ofsted school reports would suggest that the school inspection agency is less familiar with this territory. Second, the Audit Commission's practice of exhibiting the detailed quantitative evidence upon which its judgements rest is one from which Ofsted would benefit. Third, the continuing distrust in which the Chief Inspector appears to be held by many in LEAs and schools – the *Times Educational Supplement* claimed that 'Chris Woodhead is known to be a passionate opponent of LEAs' (*Times Educational Supplement*, 23 January 1998) – needs to be mediated if the value of the inspection exercise is not to be undermined by personality clashes and vituperation, as was nearly the case in the report on Birmingham LEA, whose Chief Education Officer, Professor Tim Brighouse, is frequently depicted as the arch-opponent of Woodhead.

Active intervention in LEAs which are deemed to be failing was heralded by the follow-up to the Hackney report. The Secretary of State, David Blunkett, sent in an improvement team led by a business manager who had previously been a member of the Education Association established by the previous Government to take over Hackney Downs School. The improvement team's task included advising council members on the reorganisation of the education department and the appointment of a Chief Education Officer. Even though, in the absence of legislation, this was done with the borough's consent it was almost certainly a sign of things to come. 'Zero tolerance of under-performance' will apply to LEAs just as it does to schools. The School Standards and Framework Act will give the Secretary of State statutory powers to take such action. It will be interesting to see whether and how often the power is used: the optimistic may hope that its very existence will give Ministers sufficient leverage and that central government action which appears to undermine the constitutional base of local government will be avoided.

The emphasis upon inspection and intervention at least suggests that the role of the LEA is considered to be significant by the present Government. But the positive signals about the contribution of LEAs should not be overinterpreted. It is equally noteworthy that with the help of the Standards and Effectiveness Unit the Government seems to be at least toying with an alternative model for managing the system. The national literacy and numeracy strategies, for example, which lay out detailed guidance on the teaching of these critical subjects, are managed by a network of regional directors to whom the literacy and numeracy consultants employed by LEAs are jointly accountable. Similarly, some of the Government's flagship initiatives like Education Action Zones encourage the testing of new models of management with the greater involvement of the private and voluntary sectors. During the new Government's first year neither Ministers nor senior officials have hesitated to tell LEAs that they are on trial.

The Government's ambivalence about the role of the LEA is reflected in the proposals for the reform of the framework of governance for schools. It is perhaps not surprising that the plea for a preoccupation with standards not structures, heavily emphasised among the principles upon which the schools White Paper was based, would lead to a degree of caution in overhauling the grant-maintained system. The proposals for foundation, community and voluntary schools probably go as far as possible without arousing resentment and hostility on the part of the grant-maintained sector.

However, the new decision-making structures for the planning of school places and for coordinating admissions, which involve school organisation committees and admission forums set up by the LEA, with reference to a local adjudicator appointed by the Secretary of State in the event of disagreement, are unlikely to be conducive to rapid progress either in freeing up the policy gridlock surrounding the removal of surplus places or in securing equity of access to popular schools. If the purpose is to facilitate a painless re-entry for grant-maintained schools to the LEA system, it may be worth sacrificing economy and equity, at least in the short term. That is a political judgement. But Ministers should be clear about the trade-off they are making.

The real potential in the Blair Government's policy for a resurgence of the LEA lies elsewhere. *Excellence in Schools* (DfEE, 1997a) flagged the Government's intention to establish a new feature on the local education map, the Education Action Zone. Action Zones are to be set up in areas 'with a mix of under-performing schools and the highest levels of disadvantage'. They are to be led by action forums, comprising parents, business and community representatives as well as the schools involved and the LEA. They are to encourage innovative practice in the raising of educational standards (and to be directly monitored by the Standards and Effectiveness Unit of the DfEE). The White Paper's somewhat bland comments were fleshed out later in more controversial detail: an option for governing bodies to cede their powers to the forum; the possibility of zones removing themselves from the national machinery for the negotiation of teachers' pay and conditions; and encouragement of private sector involvement, even to the extent of running schools, according to newspaper reports of a press conference held by Professor Michael Barber at the North of England Education Conference in January 1998. Some of the early publicity was confusing – are zones about innovation or compensating for failure? – and misguided. After local management, there is no going back from governing body-led school autonomy. Indeed, the announcement was interpreted by some parts of the media and by some local authorities as the thin end of a wedge which might lead to the end of a local government role in education.

Yet the concept of the zone is seminal. It compels a focus on social disadvantage, but in terms of levering up performance, not lowering expectation. It encourages cooperation among the schools in an area and could potentially be the antidote that is needed to nearly two decades of internecine competition. It offers local education authorities the opportunity to develop a wider vision of their role in lifelong learning, providing a new platform for cooperation with further and higher education, Training and Enterprise Councils and the providers of early years services. When set alongside similar initiatives promoted by other parts of the Government (Health Action Zones, Welfare to Work, Youth Offender Teams, Employment Action Zones and, above all, the establishment of a Social Exclusion Unit), it has the potential to break down the traditional barriers between services and budgets and to foster creative solutions to complex problems. And because the Government has opened up the possibility that zones might operate outside the usual constraints of national structures and machinery, they have the opportunity to respond imaginatively and flexibly to the needs of whole communities. Above all, it offers scope for local political leadership, quite distinct from the professional agenda of targets and pedagogy.

The Social Exclusion Unit, which is located within the Cabinet Office, under the Prime Minister's supervision, is clearly wrestling with the need to establish a clear agenda. But at least we now have a Government which is prepared to challenge the policy chimneys at national level. The question is whether local government is capable of responding. There is a danger that some local authorities may adopt a dog-in-the-manger attitude to change, rejecting what is proposed because of a fear of challenge to their traditional empires and perhaps anxious to protect the interests of their staff from the encroachment of the private sector. That would be a grave mistake, not only for local councils but for the communities they serve. Tony Blair, in the pamphlet he wrote on the future of local government, makes clear his expectations:

> A changing role is part of your heritage. The people's needs require you to change again so that you can play your part in helping to modernise Britain and, in partnership with others, deliver the policies on which this government was elected. If you accept this challenge, you will not find us wanting. If you are unable or unwilling to work to the modern agenda then the government will have to look to other partners to take on your role. (Blair, 1998)

However, not all the onus is on local government. The Blair administration must apply its reforming zeal to some of the long-standing impediments to local government effectiveness. The funding regime must be reformed so that local people can understand what they are buying with their council tax and more effectively hold their council to account. This applies especially to education, where the funding arrangements have become increasingly opaque: the spectacle of central and local government each blaming the other for the failure to fund the teachers' pay rise, as happened under Gillian Shephard, is both unedifying and deeply undermining of public confidence in both. If central government is minded to pursue a national funding formula for schools, then there might be a complementary local funding element to allow councils to develop local initiatives in response to the needs of their communities. The local education fund might meet the costs of, say, the council's activities in respect of raising standards; individual pupil services including special educational needs; enhancement of the curriculum through sports, the arts and the library service; and its administrative functions such as planning places and coordinating admissions.

Whatever duties local education authorities are given, it will be important that there are real decisions for them to make. It cannot be expected that people of quality will be willing to give time and energy to becoming councillors if there is no real job to do. It is up to Ministers to convince potential candidates that they are needed. The role set out in the Blair pamphlet quoted above is a good start: it is a role which should inspire courageous and visionary local politicians. The proposal for an elected Mayor of London, which seems likely to be replicated in other places, symbolises the new approach and will undoubtedly be a way of breathing new vigour into politics at the local level. Education must be a part of the local vision. Without it as a driver, the kind of transformational change which is required to give inner-city communities like those in Lambeth new hope and confidence in the future simply cannot happen. The agenda which has been set for LEAs is as demanding as it is delicate, and in pursuing it local government must not forget the painful lessons of the last decade and a half. Tony Blair's preoccupation with education and local leadership offers an unparalleled opportunity. It is an opportunity that is unlikely to be repeated.

13

CONCLUSION

CLYDE CHITTY AND JOHN DUNFORD

It is possible to argue that New Labour has accepted much of the Conservative Government's education agenda and has been content merely to modify some of its wilder excesses. The assisted places scheme has been abandoned, along with plans to extend the widely discredited nursery voucher scheme; and it is true that we have lost most of the proposals to reintroduce secondary selection outlined in the last Conservative White Paper *Self-Government for Schools*, published in June 1996 (DfEE, 1996b). But these can be seen as minor but nonetheless welcome exceptions to the rule: on a broad front, the Conservative education programme has remained remarkably intact.

CURRICULUM CHANGE

One of the most significant features of the 1988 Education Reform Act was the introduction of a National Curriculum for pupils aged 5 to 16 in all state schools in England and Wales. It was attacked by many at the time (see, for example, the various contributions to Lawton and Chitty, 1988) for its hasty implementation, its disregard of recent debates about curriculum and assessment and the lack of genuine consultation with teachers and other professionals. There was little evidence of an educational purpose or of a set of clearly worked out principles underpinning the new structure: in the memorable phrase used later by Peter Watkins, deputy chief executive of the National Curriculum Council from 1988 to 1991, 'the National Curriculum had no architect, only builders' (Watkins, 1993, p. 73). For all these reasons, it seemed highly unlikely that the National Curriculum could survive for long in its original form; and this has indeed proved to be the case. The Dearing Review of 1993 was a brave attempt to relieve the Government of some of its difficulties and, at the same time, secure a measure of professional support for a bitterly contested reform. It could not give the National Curriculum a rationale or coherence which would ensure its survival into the twenty-first century.

Now New Labour is continuing the process of dismantling initiated by the Conservatives, and this is being done on an ad hoc, piecemeal basis without any sense of contributing to a broad overall strategy or design.

In January 1998, the Government announced that pupils under the age of 11 would no longer be required to stick to the detailed national syllabuses in history, geography, design and technology, art, music and PE. Then in February, a document from the Qualifications and Curriculum Authority (QCA) informed the educational world that the Secretary of State had decided to open up major opportunities for the wider use of work-related learning at key stage 4, both *within* and *beyond* the National Curriculum. Using powers available to him under Section 363 of the 1996 Education Act, David Blunkett allowed schools to set aside the programmes of study for 14–16 year olds in up to two National Curriculum subjects, excluding English, mathematics, information technology and physical education – 'subject to criteria designed to guarantee pupils' entitlement to breadth, balance and progression'. Finally, one of the supposed 'attractions' for the consortia which will operate the Education Action Zones is that they will be granted powers to modify or abandon parts of the National Curriculum.

All this is viewed by teachers and teacher educators with mixed feelings. Eric Spear makes clear in Chapter 2 that the 1988 Education Reform Act imposed upon primary schools 'an unmanageable, subject-based curriculum'; and John Dunford argues that the arrangements for key stage 4 were equally unworkable for students at the other end of the age range. Nevertheless, what we have now lost is any sense of student 'entitlement', a concept that Tamsyn Imison appears to value in her contribution. This was a concept to which HMI attached such importance in their three Red Books (DES, 1977, 1981a and 1983a), and we are now in danger of losing it completely. We may still have a set of syllabuses for certain pupils at certain ages; but we do not have a national entitlement curriculum in any meaningful sense.

POST-16 PROVISION

Another issue where there is continuing muddle and confusion is that relating to post-16 education and training. It is no exaggeration to describe the present system as a jungle with no underpinning rationale: as John Dunford argues in Chapter 5, 'the lack of a coherent structure for 16–19 qualifications, which has been a feature of the last 20 years, remains, continuing to frustrate school curriculum planners at the end of the twentieth century'.

When Sir Ron (now Lord) Dearing and his team began work on the process of reviewing post-16 provision in 1995, they were faced with a system of at least 16,000 qualifications for 16–19 year olds – a stark reflection of decades of short-term solutions to intractable problems and a state of affairs posing very real difficulties for teachers and students alike. In the words of the ensuing report:

> What we have for 16–19 year-olds is the product of history. Initiatives have followed one another over time. Each has been designed for its own purpose, with limited concern to provide coherence and ready understanding on the part of students, parents and employers, or to provide a framework in which it is possible to combine elements from the different pathways, or to move from one pathway to related study in another . . . It is all too easy for those professionally engaged in the central administration of qualifications to overestimate the level of knowledge about the present maze of qualifications among parents and small and medium-sized employers. Even those engaged in education sometimes need help. (Dearing, 1996, p. 11)

The Dearing Report sought to accomplish the impossible task of reconciling a flexible approach to 16–19 qualifications with the maintenance of A levels as the 'gold standard'. It was committed to the idea that students should be able to follow any of three distinct 'pathways': 'academic', through GCSEs to A levels; 'applied', through GNVQ intermediate and advanced levels, taken at school or college, leading either to higher education or to employment; and 'vocational', by means of job-specific National Vocational Qualifications (NVQs) designed to 'develop and recognise mastery of a trade or profession at the relevant level'. Admittedly, it might be possible for a number of students to build up a 'portfolio of qualifications' that included qualifications from both the academic and applied pathways, but the report was anxious to emphasise the distinctiveness of the various pathways, arguing that it would be wrong to seek to build up common elements if this were to 'undermine the distinctive purposes being served by an A-level or a GNVQ'.

New Labour shows little inclination to modify radically the Dearing approach. The DfEE's consultation paper on the future of post-16 qualifications, *Qualifying for Success*, published towards the end of 1997, was intended to 'build on the Dearing reforms' and showed a marked reluctance to rethink the general direction of post-16 change. It appeared to accept the inevitability of the academic/vocational divide for older students and saw no need to tackle the problem of A levels, the examination which puts such a serious brake on the reform of 16–19 qualifications. Indeed we are assured that:

> The Labour Government is committed to GCE A-levels. A-levels allow young people to acquire a high level of knowledge and understanding in the subjects and academic disciplines which they cover. They will continue to represent the main route into higher education for 16–18 year-olds. (DfEE, 1997b, p. 12)

Above all, the new Government's approach fails to locate the problem of post-16 qualifications within the context of either comprehensive education or lifelong learning. The Government continues to allow the school curriculum to be dominated by the concepts of academic 'excellence' held by the traditional elite universities and by the selective schools.

TEACHER MORALE

New Labour has done little to restore teacher morale in this country after 18 years of negative government propaganda about incompetent teachers and failing schools. It was a grave misjudgement for former Minister of State Stephen Byers to name the 18 'worst performing schools' shortly after taking office. And it was equally foolish of Tony Blair to announce on the BBC television 'Breakfast with Frost' programme *before* the general election that Chris Woodhead would enjoy his full support as Chief Inspector of Schools in the event of a Labour victory. Such pronouncements convey a message to teachers that the Labour Government will not change the balance between pressure and support, as Tony Blair had promised before the 1997 general election.

After years of pointless conflict, a Labour victory should have heralded a new and exhilarating era of cooperation and consensus. But, as former Labour Party deputy leader, Roy Hattersley, has argued, the psychology has not changed:

> If Stephen Byers and Chris Woodhead are to have their way, schools are to be frightened into improvement by the threat of exposure. The blame is again heaped on teachers, not the conditions of deprivation in which their pupils live or the inadequate and underfunded buildings in which teachers and pupils are often required to work. Bullying teachers is the easy, as well as the cheap, option for a Secretary of State who genuinely wants improvement but has not been provided with sufficient resources to bring it about. (*Observer*, 25 May 1997)

The Government has certainly provided extra money for the education budget, but this takes time to work through to the level of the individual school, which is the point where it begins to have an effect on morale.

Martin Lawn writes in Chapter 9 that 'to speak of the teaching profession is to speak the language of the past in England'. When they are not regarded as trendy incompetents, teachers are too often regarded by government as the 'deliverers' of a new centralised curriculum which is a given. New Labour needs to understand that such a view of their work not only undermines the self-esteem and professional autonomy of teachers, but also devalues the teaching process itself. A government with a genuine belief in the professionalism of teachers would have created a General Teaching Council with the Teacher Training Agency under its control.

It is not only teacher morale which is affected by this approach to the government of education. Equally fundamentally, and more urgently, it is the supply of teachers which is being threatened. This is the single most important problem for the Government and will be solved only when young people with the best qualifications and most attractive personalities want to enter teaching in large numbers. While teachers are poorly paid, their work is regulated in detail by central agencies, and their best efforts – often in the face of horrendous social problems, as Pat Collings has emphasised in Chapter 6 – are publicly criticised, the country will not have the teaching force which it needs.

CENTRALISATION

There can be no doubt of the commitment of Education Ministers towards state education. David Blunkett's sons have attended state schools in

Sheffield, where he used to be chair of the city's Education Committee; Estelle Morris was a teacher in comprehensive schools, including the inner-city Sidney Stringer School in Coventry; Stephen Byers was chair of North Tyneside Education Committee. This represents a marked contrast with the views and experience of Mark Carlisle and Keith Joseph, quoted in Chapter 1. David Blunkett's own background as a pupil at a school for the blind was very unsatisfactory and, if he had taken the advice of his headteacher, he would have been destined for one of the careers traditionally associated with blind people, rather than the successful political career which he has had. This personal experience has given him a fierce determination to ensure that no young person suffers from low expectations of teachers or from a poor standard of education. His commitment to the life chances of young people, particularly those with special educational needs, is absolute. Yet Blunkett knows that Education Ministers since the Second World War have, on average, served for only two and a half years and therefore he is a Minister in a hurry. The two Education Bills, published early in the Government's term of office, covered a huge agenda and required a very large legislative programme. As the Conservative Government discovered when it introduced the National Curriculum and many other measures in the Education Reform Act of 1988, a government in a hurry makes mistakes when it tries to legislate on too many issues at one time. Between a White Paper and an Education Act, there is too little time to consult thoroughly about all the details of new measures if too many are introduced simultaneously. The devil, from the school's – and subsequently if things go wrong, from the Government's – viewpoint, is in the detail and this often takes time to become apparent.

A further problem in too much simultaneous legislation is that it takes time to institutionalise change in schools. Effective change comes not through government diktat but through what actually happens in thousands of classrooms across the country. We do not doubt David Blunkett's passion for education, nor his commitment to raise standards of achievement; but there is a clear danger that too much legislation, too quickly introduced, will not reach down to classroom level in the way he intends.

There have traditionally been two ways in which this problem can be addressed. Either the teachers can be persuaded of the wisdom of the Government's policies and then trusted to deliver its programme or the Government can exercise greater central control over the education system and insist, through external inspection and other pressure, that the policies are carried out. It seems that the Labour Government, like its predecessor, has chosen the second course of action.

THE THIRD WAY

A major omission in the programme of the Labour Government is its failure to undo many of the measures which stemmed from the marketplace philosophy of the previous Government and which created a culture of competition in education at all levels. Instead of accelerating the search for an agreed set of measures of school performance, the 'league tables' have continued largely in their previous form and the basis on which schools are financed has remained unchanged. Culture cannot be changed in a week, or even a year, but it is to be hoped that the Government introduces measures which move the school system from a culture of competition to a culture of cooperation.

We hear much talk of Tony Blair and his colleagues pursuing 'the Third Way' in their political and social programme. This is said to be the ultimate modernising project which will enable Britain to thrive and prosper in the next millennium. But what exactly does it entail as far as education is concerned?

Part of the answer was provided by Stephen Byers in a lecture delivered to the Social Market Foundation in London in July 1998. Central to the new philosophy was apparently the setting up of a network of Education Action Zones, designed to tackle 'endemic levels of low achievement and low expectations'. In the words of the former Schools Minister:

> The Education Action Zones contain many proposals that would have been regarded as impossible to achieve just 12 months ago – performance-related pay for teachers; ditching the National Curriculum to focus on key skills and work-related learning; masterclasses on devolved budgets for governing bodies run by some of the world's leading financial consultants; provision to identify and stretch the most able pupils; agreed working on Saturdays and during school holidays. (reprinted in the *Independent*, 2 July 1998)

From all this, it seems clear that the Third Way in education is about far more than simply stretching pupils and raising school standards. It is, as many critics fear, about marginalising local education authorities and introducing a degree of privatisation. It is, when all is said and done, a fine phrase designed to disguise an underlying continuity between New Labour and Thatcherism.

NOTES ON CONTRIBUTORS

Clyde Chitty is professor of education at Goldsmiths College, London. He has taught at the University of Birmingham and at the Institute of Education, London. Before that, he was vice-principal and then acting principal of a community college in Leicestershire. He is co-editor of the educational journal *Forum.*

Pat Collings was for 13 years head of Sinfin Community School in the city of Derby. She is a former publications officer of the Secondary Heads Association and was a member of its Executive and Council. She was the subject of 'A Head's Tale' (BBC 2, 1995). She is now an education management consultant and an assessor for the National Professional Qualification for Headteachers.

Peter Downes was head of Hinchingbrooke School, Huntingdon, one of the first schools to undertake local management of schools, from 1982 to 1996. He was president of the Secondary Heads Association in 1994/5. He is now an educational consultant specialising in school management, finance and school improvement.

John Dunford is general secretary of the Secondary Heads Association, of which he was president from 1995/6. From 1982 to 1998 he was head of Durham Johnston Comprehensive School. He is an honorary research fellow at Durham University.

Heather Du Quesnay was director of education for Hertfordshire from 1991–94. She is a past president of the Society of Education Officers and is currently executive director of education for the London Borough of Lambeth.

Robert Godber is head of Wath-upon-Dearne Comprehensive School, Rotherham. He is a former publications officer of the Secondary Heads Association and is a member of its Executive and Council.

Dame Tamsyn Imison is head of Hampstead School in the London Borough of Camden. She was a member of the Council and Executive of the Secondary Heads Association.

Martin Lawn is reader in education at Westhill College, Birmingham, and visiting professor of education at Umea University, Sweden.

Roger Seckington was a principal of three Leicestershire Community Colleges during 1970–93 and is now retired and living in Dorset.

Eric Spear is head of Staplehurst County Primary School, Tonbridge, Kent. He is a member of the Council of the National Association of Headteachers.

BIBLIOGRAPHY

Aldrich, R. (1996), *Education for the Nation.* London, Institute of Education, University of London.

Alexander, W. (1954), *Education in England: the National System and How it Works*. London, Newnes.

Archer, J. (1998), *A Better Deal for London*. London, Centre for Policy Studies.

Association for Colleges, Association of Principals of Sixth Form Colleges, Girls' Schools Association, Headmasters' Conference, Secondary Heads Association, Society of Headmasters and Headmistresses in Independent Schools (1994), *Post-Compulsory Education and Training*. London, AfC *et al.*

Association of Chief Education Officers (1997), *LEA Framework for External Reviews.* London, ACEO.

Audit Commission (1991), *Management within Primary Schools.* London, HMSO.

Audit Commission (1997), *Trading Places.* London, Audit Commission.

Audit Commission (1998), *Changing Partners*. London, Audit Commission.

Auld, R. (1976), *William Tyndale Junior and Infants Schools Public Inquiry: A Report to the Inner London Education Authority by Robin Auld QC*. London, Inner London Education Authority.

Barber, M. (1996), *The National Curriculum: A Study in Policy*. Keele, Keele University Press.

Barnes, A. (1983), 'Undergoing a Formal Inspection – What It Was Like', *Education*, 20 May, 391.

Bayliss, V. (1998), *Redefining Work.* London, Royal Society of Arts.

Benn, C. and Chitty, C. (1996), *Thirty Years On: Is Comprehensive Education Alive and Well or Struggling to Survive?* (1st edn). London, David Fulton.

Benn, C. and Simon, B. (1972), *Half Way There: Report on the British Comprehensive School Reform* (2nd edn). London, Penguin Books.

Blair, A. (1998), *Leading the Way: A New Vision for Local Government.* London, Institute for Public Policy Research.

Bowring-Carr, C. (1996), 'Inspecting by the Book', in J. Ouston, P. Earley and B. Fidler (eds), *OFSTED Inspections: The Early Experience.* London, David Fulton.

Bridges, D., and McLaughlin, T.H. (eds), (1994), *Education and the Market Place.* London, Falmer Press.

Brimblecombe, N., Ormston, M. and Shaw, M. (1995), 'Teachers' Perceptions of School Inspection: A Stressful Experience', *Cambridge Journal of Education,* xxv (1), 1995, 109–16.

Browne, S. (1979), 'The Accountability of HM Inspectorate (England)', in J. Lello (ed.), *Accountability in Education.* London, Ward Lock Educational.

Burns, T. (1977), *The BBC: Public Institution and Private World.* London, Tavistock.

Bush, T., Coleman, M. and Glover, D. (1993), *Managing Autonomous Schools: the Grant-Maintained Experience.* London, Paul Chapman.

Chitty, C. (1989), *Towards a New Education System: the Victory of the New Right?* London, Falmer Press.

Chitty, C. (1992), *The Education System Transformed.* Manchester, Baseline Books.

Chitty, C. (1997), 'Interview with Keith Joseph', in P. Ribbins and B. Sherratt (eds), *Conservative Secretaries of State and Radical Educational Reform since 1979.* London, Cassell.

Davis, C. (1996), 'The Early Experience of OFSTED', in J. Ouston, P. Earley and B. Fidler (eds), *OFSTED Inspections: The Early Experience.* London, David Fulton.

Dearing, R. (1994), *A Review of the National Curriculum.* London, School Curriculum and Assessment Authority.

Dearing, R. (1996), *Review of Qualifications for 16–19 Year Olds.* London, School Curriculum and Assessment Authority.

Department of Education and Science (1967), *Children and their Primary Schools* (the Plowden Report), 2 vols. London, HMSO.

Department of Education and Science (1977), *Curriculum 11–16* (HMI Red Book 1). London, HMSO.

Department of Education and Science (1978), *Primary Education in England: A Survey by HM Inspectors of Schools.* London, HMSO.

Department of Education and Science (1979), *Aspects of Secondary Education in England.* London, HMSO.

Department of Education and Science (1980a), *A Framework for the School Curriculum.* London, HMSO.

Department of Education and Science (1980b), *HMI Report on Education Provision by the Inner London Education Authority.* London, HMSO.

Department of Education and Science (1981a), *Curriculum 11–16: a Review of Progress* (HMI Red Book 2). London, HMSO.

Department of Education and Science (1981b), *The School Curriculum.* London, HMSO.

Department of Education and Science (1983a), *Curriculum 11–16: Towards a*

Statement of Entitlement: Curricular Reappraisal in Action (HMI Red Book 3). London, HMSO.
Department of Education and Science (1983b), *HM Inspectors Today: Standards in Education*. London, HMSO.
Department of Education and Science (1985), *Better Schools*. London, HMSO.
Department of Education and Science (1988), *Advancing A Levels* (the Higginson Report). London, HMSO.
Department of Education and Science (1989), *Standards in Education 1987–88: The Annual Report of HM Senior Chief Inspector of Schools*. London, HMSO.
Department for Education (1992), *Choice and Diversity: A New Framework for Schools*. London, HMSO.
Department for Education (1992), *HMI Report on Non Teaching Staff in Schools*. London, HMSO.
Department for Education and Employment (1996a), *Learning to Compete: Education and Training for 14–19 Year Olds*. London, HMSO.
Department for Education and Employment (1996b), *Self-Government for Schools*: London, HMSO.
Department for Education and Employment (1997a), *Excellence in Schools*: London, HMSO.
Department for Education and Employment (1997b), *Qualifying for Success: A Consultation Paper on the Future of post-16 Qualifications*. London, DfEE.
Department for Education and Employment (1998), *Code of Practice on LEA–School Relations, Draft for Consultation*. London, DfEE.
Dunford, J. (1997a), *Curriculum 2000+*. Leicester, Secondary Heads Association.
Dunford, J. (1997b), 'Bridging the Divide: A Vision for the Future', *Forum*, xxxix (3), Autumn.
Dunford, J. (1998), *Her Majesty's Inspectorate of Schools Since 1944: Standard Bearers or Turbulent Priests?* London, Woburn.
Graham, D. and Tytler, D. (1993), *A Lesson for Us All: The Making of the National Curriculum*: London, Routledge.
Graham D. (1996), *The Education Racket*. Glasgow, Neil Wilson.
Gray, J. and Hannon, V. (1986), 'HMI's Interpretation of Schools' Examination Results', *Journal of Education Policy*, 1, 23–33.
Hargreaves, D. (1984), *Report on Improving Secondary Schools*. London, ILEA.
Hodgson, A. and Spours, K. (eds) (1997), *Dearing and Beyond: 14–19 Qualifications, Frameworks and Systems*. London, Kogan Page.
Howarth, S. (ed.) (1999), *Head's Legal Guide*. Kingston-upon-Thames, Croner.
Hussain, F. and Hughes, A. (1995), 'A Comprehensive Community College', *Forum*, ii, 52–4.
Inner London Education Authority (1983), *Race, Sex and Class*, 3 vols:
1. Achievement in Schools. London, ILEA.
2. Multi-Ethnic Education in Schools. London, ILEA.
3. A Policy for Equality: Race. London ILEA.
Institute for Public Policy Research (IPPR) (1990), *A British Baccalaureat: Ending the Division between Education and Training*. London, IPPR.
Jones, D. (1988), *Stewart Mason. The Art of Education*. London, Lawrence &

Wishart.
Kennedy, H. (1998), *Learning Pays* (the Kennedy Report). London, HMSO.
Kerckhoff, A.C., Fogelman, K., Crook, D. and Reeder, D. (1996), *Going Comprehensive in England and Wales: A Study of Uneven Change*. London, Woburn Press.
Kidd, L. (1991), *16–19: The Way Forward*. Leicester, Secondary Heads Association.
Kidd, L. (1992), *16–19: Towards a Coherent System*. Leicester, Secondary Heads Association.
Knight, C. (1990), *The Making of Tory Education Policy in Post-War Britain, 1950–1986*. London, Falmer Press.
Labour Party (1995), *Diversity and Excellence: A New Partnership for Schools*. London, Labour Party.
Lash, S. and Urry, J. (1994), *Economies of Signs and Spaces*. London, Sage.
Lawn, M. (1995), 'Restructuring Teaching in the USA and England: Moving Towards the Differentiated, Flexible Leader', *Journal of Education Policy*, x (4), 347–60.
Lawton, D. (1993), 'Is there Coherence and Purpose in the National Curriculum?' in C. Chitty and B. Simon (eds), *Education Answers Back: Critical Responses to Government Policy*. London, Lawrence & Wishart.
Lawton, D. (1997), 'What is Worth Learning?', in R. Pring and G. Walford, *Affirming the Comprehensive Ideal*. London, Falmer.
Lawton, D. and Chitty, C. (eds) (1988), *The National Curriculum*, Bedford Way Paper 33. London, Institute of Education, University of London.
Learmonth, J. (ed.) (1993), *Teaching and Learning in Cities*. London, Whitbread in the Community.
Lester Smith, W.O. (1945), *To Whom Do Schools Belong?* Oxford, Basil Blackwell.
Macfarlane, E. (1993), *Education 16–19: In Transition*. London, Routledge & Kegan Paul.
Macgilchrist, B., Myers, K. and Reed, J. (1997), *The Intelligent School*. London, Paul Chapman.
Major, J. (1991), *Citizen's Charter*. London, HMSO.
Mandelson, P. and Liddle, R. (1996), *The Blair Revolution: Can New Labour Deliver?* London, Faber & Faber.
Mortimore, P., Mortimore, J. and Thomas, H. (1993), *The Innovative Uses of Non-Teaching Staff in Primary and Secondary Schools*. London, HMSO.
Mortimore, P., Sammons P., Stoll, L., Lewis, D. and Ecob, R. (1988), *School Matters*. London, Open Books.
National Commission on Education (1993), *Learning to Succeed: A Radical Look at Education Today and A Strategy for the Future*. London, Heinemann.
Office for Standards in Education (Ofsted) (1992; 2nd edn, 1995), *Framework for the Inspection of Schools*. London, Ofsted.
Ouston, J., Earley, P. and Fidler, B. (eds), (1996), *Ofsted Inspections: The Early Experience*. London, David Fulton.
Patten, J. (1992), 'Who's Afraid of the "S" Word?', *New Statesman and Society*, 17 July, 20–1.

Perkin, H. (1989), *The Rise of Professional Society: England since 1880.* London, Routledge & Kegan Paul.

Plaskow, M. (1990), 'It Was the Best of Times', *Education*, 3 August.

Ranson, S. and Stewart, J. (1994), *Management for the Public Domain: Enabling the Learning Society*. London, Macmillan.

Ribbins, P. and Sherratt, B. (1997), *Conservative Secretaries of State and Radical Educational Reform since 1973.* London, Cassell.

Rubinstein, D. and Simon, B. (1973), *The Evolution of the Comprehensive School, 1926–1972.* London, Routledge & Kegan Paul.

Ruddock, J., Chaplain, R. and Wallace, G. (eds) (1996), *School Improvement – What Can Pupils Tell Us?* London, David Fulton.

Sallis, J. (1998), *Schools, Parents and Governors: A New Approach to Accountability*. London, Routledge & Kegan Paul.

School Curriculum and Assessment Authority (1995), *Managing the Curriculum at Key Stage 4.* London, SCAA.

Scottish Office Education Department (SOED) (1994), *Higher Still.* London: HMSO.

Secondary Heads Association (SHA) (1983), *A View from the Bridge.* Leicester, SHA.

Secondary Heads Association (1987), *Future Imperative: A View of 14–18 and Beyond.* Leicester, SHA.

Secondary Heads Association (1993), *14–19: Pathways to Achievement.* Leicester, SHA.

Secondary Heads Association (1996), *Towards More Effective Schools: Secondary School Inspections Beyond 1997.* Leicester, SHA.

Street, P. (1997), *Managing Schools in the Community*. London, Arena.

Tomlinson, H. (ed.), (1993), *Education and Training 14–19: Continuity and Diversity in the Curriculum.* London, Longman.

Tomlinson, S. (1997), 'A Comprehensive Curriculum 14–19', in R. Pring and G. Walford, *Affirming the Comprehensive Ideal.* London, Falmer, pp. 109–18.

Walford, G. and Jones, S. (1986), 'The Solihull Adventure: An Attempt to Reintroduce Selective Schooling', *Journal of Education Policy*, 1(3) (July), 239–53.

Watkins, P. (1993), 'The National Curriculum – An Agenda for the Nineties', in C. Chitty and B. Simon (eds), *Education Answers Back: Critical Responses to Government Policy*. London, Lawrence & Wishart.

Webb, S. (1918), *The Teacher in Politics*. London, Fabian Society.

White, J.P. (1973), *Towards a Compulsory Curriculum.* London, Routledge & Kegan Paul.

Wiseman, S. and Pidgeon, D. (1970), *Curriculum Evaluation*. Slough, National Foundation for Educational Research.

Woodhead, C. (1995), *A Question of Standards: Finding the Balance*. London, Politeia.

Young, H. (1989), *One of Us: A Biography of Margaret Thatcher*. London, Macmillan.

INDEX

Lightning Source UK Ltd.
Milton Keynes UK
16 February 2011

167626UK00001B/55/P

9 780713 040340